WHY SHOULD "I" SPEAK IN TONGUES???

by Charles ♥ Frances Hunter

published by
Hunter Ministries Publishing Company
1602 Townhurst
Houston, Texas 77043

Canadian Office

Hunter Ministries Publishing Company of Canada
G-9, Station 9
Calgary, Alberta, Canada T3A-2G1

Copyright 1976 by Charles and Frances Hunter, all rights reserved. Published by Hunter Ministries Publishing Company, 1602 Townhurst, Houston, Texas 77043. Printed in U.S.A.

Scripture quotations are taken from:

The Authorized King James Version (KJV)

The Living Bible, Paraphrased. Tyndale House Publishers, Wheaton, Illinois, 1971. All references not specified are from the Living Bible.

Revised Standard Version (RSV), Zondervan Publishing House, Inc.

OTHER HUNTER BOOKS

COME ALIVE
DELIGHTFULLY CHARISMATIC Christian
    Walk Seminar Manual
DON'T LIMIT GOD
FOLLOW ME
GOD IS FABULOUS
GOD'S ANSWER TO FAT . . . LOØSE IT!
HOT LINE TO HEAVEN
HOW TO MAKE YOUR MARRIAGE EXCITING
IMPOSSIBLE MIRACLES
IT'S SO SIMPLE
    formerly HANG LOOSE WITH JESUS
LET'S GO WITNESSING
    formerly GO, MAN, GO
MY LOVE AFFAIR WITH CHARLES
NUGGETS OF TRUTH
P.T.L.A. (Praise the Lord, Anyway!)
SINCE JESUS PASSED BY
the fabulous SKINNIE MINNIE RECIPE BOOK
THIS WAY UP↑
TWO SIDES OF THE COIN

TABLE OF CONTENTS

INTRODUCTION 7
W. AUSTIN WILKERSON 15
SHIRLEY NORWOOD 35
DR. JERRY AND ANN HORNER 51
BARBARA JEAN SONNTAG 77
MILTON L. HAMON 85
JACK AND JEAN WOOD 95
A.L. AND JOYCE GILL 103
JERRY WOODFILL 119
DR. STEPHEN AND ROSE GYLAND 129
BOB MURPHY 137
DR. HONG AND AMY SIT 145
DR. W. DOUGLAS FOWLER, JR. 157
WHO, HOW AND WHY? 183

INTRODUCTION

Jesus, the most beautiful gift that was ever given to the world, contained ALL of God in a tiny human body the moment he was born. God loved the world sufficiently to let this child he loved so much die on a cross for us! God did more for the human race in giving us Jesus than anything that has ever been accomplished by scientists, educators, teachers, or all things combined.

The Pharisees condemned him! They said he was of the devil! They credited his power to the devil. They said this about the Savior of the world!

That's hard to imagine, isn't it? Or is it?

The most beautiful gift Jesus sent back to the world was the gift which he planned to go hand in hand with salvation. When he went to heaven, he sent back the Holy Spirit to accompany God's original gift of salvation. He sent back the Holy Spirit to give us power to live the Christian life. The baptism of the Holy Spirit is as natural as salvation and as normal for a Christian as accepting Jesus as the Savior of the world.

It is difficult to believe that the same things are being said today of the beautiful gift of the Holy Spirit as were said about Jesus. Gordon Lindsay says: "To say that all supernatural manifestations of the speaking in tongues in general are the work of evil spirits is to take a daring and dangerous stand. The Pharisees were the fundamentalists of Christ's day, and they attributed his works to the power of the devil (Matt. 12:22-30). Jesus not only rebuked such accusations but said, '. . . All manner of sin and blasphemy shall be forgiven unto men: but the blasphemy against the Holy Ghost shall not be forgiven unto men.' (Matt. 12:31) KJV"

The beautiful gift of power to the Christian world has been lambasted, condemned, forbidden, ridiculed and criticized by the Pharisees of the 20th century, as they attribute the work of God's Holy Spirit to the devil, claiming that Jesus has changed and is not the same as he was 2,000 years ago. Some attempt to negate the healing power of the Holy Spirit today; some insist that speaking in tongues is of the devil. Some refuse to believe that miracles are occurring when people fall under the power. Some do not accept prophecy, messages in tongues and interpretations.

The Bible will always stand the test if we believe the Bible is true! THERE'S NOTHING IN THE BIBLE THAT EVER MENTIONS THE DEVIL AND TONGUES! The only time that tongues are ever mentioned in the word of God is in conjunction with the Holy Spirit! We never have to worry about criticism when we stand on the word of God! The best proof of the baptism of the Holy Spirit is a life of intimacy with God and a walk in the power of the Spirit.

It IS genuine, it IS real, and it IS for today! The most exciting people we know are the ones who have accepted the baptism of the Holy Spirit! People whose every word, thought and deed concerns Jesus. People whose lives overflow with the fruit of the Spirit! Many people are opposed to Charismatics because they feel too much emphasis has been put upon speaking in tongues. This is interesting, because the only proof the Bible offers concerning the baptism of the Holy Spirit is SPEAKING IN TONGUES!

The first time "tongues" were ever mentioned in the Bible was by Jesus himself! In the 16th chapter of Mark, where Jesus was speaking to his disciples, he made some very emphatic statements! Many people feel the Great Commission of the Bible appears in the last chapter of Matthew. The COMPLETE Great Commission appears in the last chapter of Mark. In this area Mark was more wordy

INTRODUCTION

than Matthew, because he included ALL of the things Jesus said about what he expected from the believers!

Notice that Jesus is talking to BELIEVERS. He says this several times in this section of the Bible. Starting with verse 15 (TLB), "And then he told them, 'You are to go into all the world and preach the Good News to everyone, everywhere. Those who BELIEVE and are baptized will be saved. But those who refuse to believe will be condemned.' " Do you know that everyone will agree with you concerning the first sentence? That's why we have missionaries from every denomination all over the world, but a lot of churches refuse to accept the second part.

I (Frances) remember when I was "saved" I was so excited about it that I ran back to the pastor of the church where I was a member and told him about my fabulous "born again" experience! He patted me on the head like I was a naughty little girl and said, "That's all right for you, honey, if you need it! " EVERYONE NEEDS IT according to my Bible!

Jesus continued talking to believers. He doesn't mention a thing about speaking to unbelievers at this point! He continued: " 'And those who believe shall use my authority to cast out demons, AND THEY SHALL SPEAK NEW LANGUAGES.' " This is as much a part of the Great Commission as the first part about preaching the gospel. Jesus didn't separate it as something for just a few people; he said it was for ALL believers!

He continued on, and this is the part that probably throws most people who do not understand it. " 'They will be able even to handle snakes with safety, and if they drink anything poisonous, it won't hurt them;' " Who wants to go out and handle snakes? We certainly don't! And we're equally sure that God doesn't intend for you to go out and put your hand in a basket of rattlesnakes just to see whether or not they bite you. What does it mean, then? Do you remember what happened to Paul when he was shipwrecked? In Acts 28:3-5 he picked up a serpent BY ACCIDENT, and he did not run around telling everyone, "Look at me, look at me, I can handle snakes with safety." No, he just shook it off into the fire and praised God because he protected him.

We certainly don't intend to go around drinking poison just to prove that we're immune, because we believe we'd soon find out we're not! God doesn't intend for us to tempt him, but his protective covering is there IF we need it. Do you notice the Bible says "IF" we (accidentally) drink anything poisonous, it won't hurt us! Hallelujah! Best insurance policy we know of!

From Genesis to Revelation, who's the biggest snake of all? SATAN, of course! And what does the baptism of the Holy Spirit do for you? It gives you the power to handle Satan because we certainly wouldn't want to argue with Satan without the power of the Holy Spirit. Before we received the baptism, we didn't believe that demons existed today! We just ignored them. The devil didn't have to worry about us because we didn't have any power to stand up against him before the baptism. Today we KNOW they're real and that they do exist in the 20th century. But praise God you've got the power to handle demons and the devil himself when you've got the power of God in your life!

Jesus didn't stop there, but continued on, giving the fifth part of the Great Commission: " 'and they will be able to place their hands on the sick and heal them.' " Jesus didn't say that just a few would be able to lay hands on the sick and heal them, he very emphatically said that ALL BELIEVERS would be able to lay hands on the sick and heal them.

Mark concluded by saying what would happen to believers when they fulfilled 100% of the Great Commission. "When the Lord Jesus had finished talking with them, he was taken up into heaven and sat down at God's

INTRODUCTION 11

right hand. And the disciples went everywhere preaching, and the Lord was with them and confirmed what they said by the miracles that followed their messages." Jesus didn't promise this to those who proclaim one out of the five parts of the Great Commission; he only promised it to those who fulfilled ALL of it:
1. Preaching the gospel
2. Using Jesus' authority to cast out demons
3. Speaking new languages
4. Handling snakes (Satan) (poison)
5. Healing the sick

Maybe you've heard that this part of Mark does not belong in the Bible, but every Bible we have in our house contains this text, and every Bible we've ever seen contains this text! And we've never seen anyone who actually cut it out of their Bible. They just ignore it!

The Bible so beautifully shows us how we are able to identify the believers who are filled with the Holy Spirit! Let's go back to the original Day of Pentecost to find the evidence: Jesus had given his disciples the Great Commission of the Bible when he told them to GO into all the world, and then promptly told them NOT TO GO, but to wait until they received power from on high.

"Seven weeks had gone by since Jesus' death and resurrection, and the Day of Pentecost had now arrived. As the believers met together that day, suddenly there was a sound like the roaring of a mighty windstorm in the skies above them and it filled the house where they were meeting. Then, what looked like flames or tongues of fire appeared and settled on their heads. And everyone present was filled with the Holy Spirit and began speaking in languages they didn't know, for the Holy Spirit gave them this ability." Acts 2:1-4 (TLB)

Isn't God unique? Who else would have thought of putting flames or tongues of fire on the heads of everyone present? I wonder who peeked first to see the flames of fire! Maybe Peter, the impetuous one? Or was it Thomas, the doubter, who might not have believed what he heard! Regardless of who it was, the Bible says they ALL began to speak in languages they didn't know. Not just some of them, but ALL of them! Hallelujah!

In Acts 8:17 (TLB) the Bible says, "Then Peter and John laid their hands upon these believers, and they received the Holy Spirit." What was it that happened that caused Simon to offer money to buy the power to lay hands on people's heads to have them receive the Holy Spirit? Surely something must have happened to cause him to want this power. Could it have been the supernatural manifestation of speaking in languages they didn't know?

Acts 10:44 (TLB) "Even as Peter was saying these things, the Holy Spirit fell upon all those listening! The Jews who came with Peter were amazed that the gift of the Holy Spirit would be given to the Gentiles too!" How did he know? Could he tell by just looking at them? No, the Bible specifically says they gave the evidence of having received, "But there could be no doubt about it, for they heard them speaking in tongues and praising God." This was 10 years after the Holy Spirit had fallen on the Day of Pentecost. IT WAS STILL GOING ON!

In the 19th chapter of Acts, verse 2, (TLB) the same thing happened! Paul arrived in Ephesus where he found several disciples! He was not talking to unbelievers, HE WAS TALKING TO DISCIPLES! He asked the famous question, " 'Did you receive the Holy Spirit when you believed?' he asked them. 'No,' they replied, 'we don't know what you mean. What is the Holy Spirit?' 'Then what beliefs did you acknowledge at your baptism?' he asked. And they replied, 'What John the Baptist taught.' Then Paul pointed out to them that John's baptism was to demonstrate a desire to turn from sin to God and that those receiving his baptism must then go on to believe in Jesus, the one John said would come later. As soon as they heard

INTRODUCTION

this, they were baptized in the name of the Lord Jesus. Then, when Paul laid his hands upon their heads, the Holy Spirit came on them, and they SPOKE IN OTHER LANGUAGES AND PROPHESIED."

Exactly the same thing happened 25 years after the Day of Pentecost! They received the Holy Spirit with exactly the same evidence as the believers did in the upper room. All of them were gathered there in one accord and ALL began speaking in tongues, and 25 years later, exactly the same thing happened again!

In the 20th century we don't have to settle for any less than the disciples did! God is pouring out his Holy Spirit in the same manner today as he did then. There is no difference. Probably the verse we've heard quoted more than any other is Hebrews 13:8, "Jesus Christ is the same yesterday, today, and forever." (TLB) If he baptized with the evidence of speaking in tongues yesterday, then surely he's doing the same thing today and will continue doing it tomorrow. The New Testament has not been rewritten since the days of the disciples and we would be assuming it had been if we are to have a different evidence (or lack of positive evidence). Every word of the New Testament was written by those who had received the baptism of the Holy Spirit and who spoke in tongues. God considered it vital. Jesus commanded it. We accepted it. It works!

In our lives very few miracles followed our enthusiastic messages as we shared the Good News, until we accepted the baptism of the Holy Spirit and spoke in tongues. We did ONE of the five parts of the Great Commission (preach the Good News) and tried to do a second part (heal the sick) but with virtually no success; the other three parts were bypassed without our awareness. Today, empowered by the Holy Spirit, our ministry has changed considerably! After we proclaim the Good News we have been privileged to see miracles occur!

We've heard it said that tongues were given on the

Day of Pentecost because there were men there from all different countries and they heard the "message" in their own language. This isn't true according to the Bible!! They heard all those in the upper room praising God in their new tongues, but the evangelist who gave the "message" spoke in only one language. Peter delivered the message that day. The Bible says he preached a long sermon, and obviously he could not talk in more than one language at a time, so he preached in whatever his native tongue was, just as we would speak in our country in our native tongue, English! And the listeners were saved by listening to his evangelistic message spoken in his native tongue. Tongues were spoken by all to praise God and tell in various languages about the mighty miracles of God — then came Peter explaining and his sermon caused 3,000 to believe.

The thing we enjoy the most about the people who have accepted the baptism with the Holy Spirit is their love of Jesus! They don't want to talk about anything else. The Holy Spirit was sent to magnify Jesus, and praise Jesus; that's exactly what he does when you are filled with the Holy Spirit!

We've met many exciting people since we received the baptism with the Holy Spirit . . . people from all walks of life and all denominations who found a new dimension in their life through the baptism of the Holy Spirit. We've asked a few of them to share with you what the baptism has done in their life, and to tell you the answer they found to "Why Should 'I' Speak in Tongues??"

May the Spirit of God speak to your heart through these stories, each one different, and each one unique in its own way, but all ending up saying exactly the same thing, just as Matthew, Mark, Luke and John did when they wrote the gospels!

W. AUSTIN WILKERSON
Pastor, Evangelistic Temple
Houston, Texas

"The baptism of the Holy Spirit is not some sort of a shelter you get in from the battle. It's giving you a gun and putting something in you that says, 'I'm going to go out and fight the devil wherever he is.'"

We were praying about the opening chapter of this book because we wanted to acquaint our readers with the Charismatic move if they had not yet been swept into it.

We went to church Sunday morning before starting to write that afternoon. God arranged at exactly the right time and on one of our rare times to be home on Sunday, for our beloved pastor to present his views on the Charismatic Renewal. We captured his beautiful presentation on cassette tape and it was exactly what we wished we could have said.

Pastor Wilkerson is recognized widely throughout the United States and other parts of the world as being solid in his understanding of the word of God. He has long been in the Pentecostal movement, but he got caught up in the new move of the Holy Spirit and became a Charismatic too!

He attended Tulsa University and graduated from the Central Bible College in Springfield, Mo. He received the Alumnus of the Year Award in 1973, the only pastor who has ever received one from CBC.

Pastor Wilkerson has been pastoring in Houston 25 years. In August of 1966, two churches merged and became Evangelistic Temple, where he has been pastoring ever since. Evangelistic Temple is one of the most exciting, people-packed, power-packed, fastest growing churches in America.

There's a lot of question and a lot of controversy right now being raised about what is called the Charismatic Renewal. I would like to share with you what I see from the Bible as it relates to this subject.

To help us understand what we're talking about, I would like first of all to establish WHAT IS the Charismatic Renewal. Why is there so much controversy? Why has almost every major denomination had to come to some conclusions relative to this subject of the Charismatic Renewal?

First of all, let's find out what "charismatic" means. The word "charismatic" comes from a Greek word "charisma." We're hearing the word "charisma" used a lot of today, not only in the religious realm or the Christian realm but also in the secular realm. You'll hear people talking about somebody having a lot of "charisma." I'd like to give you Mr. Webster's definition of "charisma." Here's what he says. I'm going to read it verbatim, so that we can know exactly what we're talking about from an official standpoint, such as Mr. Webster.

"A special divine or spiritual gift, a special divine endowment conferred upon a believer as an evidence of the experience of divine grace and fitting him for the life, work, or office to which he was called. A grace (and if you understand what the word 'grace' means, it is an unmerited favor of God) as a miraculously given power of healing or of speaking in tongues or of prophesying, etc., attributed to some of the early Christians." Mr. Webster says that "charismatic" or "charisma" or "charismata" means a divine endowment to enable a believer or a person to carry out the life or the office to which a believer has been called. When we come to the subject of "Charismatic Renewal" this is a problem, because most Christian people who believe in church history at all will conclude that all of these things have happened in the past. They know because the Bible says that it happened, that there was a special day, the Day of Pentecost, which most churches conclude was the beginning of the Christian Church, and that this was also an experience that happened often and regularly in the days of the apostles, that it was part of the early day Christian Church.

The problem is the subject of the "Charismatic Renewal," which means a renewal NOW of the divine enablement or gifts of the Spirit to the church. Many people believe in the historical outpouring of God's Holy Spirit. They believe that God sent to the early apostles this special enablement to thrust the church into a profitable, effective ministry in their generation.

For nearly 2,000 years the church (off and on) has had spiritual awakenings, spiritual renewal, or as we call it "revival." The question is, "Is the Charismatic Renewal that we are seeing today scripturally in order with the Bible?" Let me go a little beyond the definition of the "charismatic" and "charismatic renewal" to point to you the origin and where it all began.

In Joel, chapter 2, verse 28 (KJV) back in the Old Testament before Jesus came, one of the prophets of God said, "... I will pour out my spirit upon all flesh." Then he goes on to say, " ... and your sons and your daughters shall prophesy." Hold onto the word "prophesy" because this is part of the divine enablement of the gifts of the Spirit or the helps, as we often refer to them. He says, "I will pour out my spirit . . . and your sons and your daughters shall prophesy." Then he goes on to explain that there will be visions and there will be dreams, and that upon the handmaids and upon the servants God would pour out his Spirit.

In the Old Testament, when the Holy Spirit came he did not come upon ALL flesh. The Holy Spirit did not come upon the general Old Testament congregation of Israel. The Holy Spirit came upon men like Elijah and Elisha, perhaps even like Enoch and upon a king like David or even upon King Saul. The Holy Spirit came upon the judges. It was an endowment or an enduement of power that made these Old Testament prophets effective. It happened on rare occasions or upon occasions where God was projecting to his people, Israel. Before the Old Testament dispensation, or the dispensation of Law (the method through which God was dealing with the world, with the people of Israel) was to come to a close, God said through one of the prophets, there will come a time when "I will pour out my spirit upon ALL flesh." This is in contrast to the fact that he only came upon the kings and the prophets and the judges, basically, in the Old Testament.

In the gospel of Mark, chapter 16, verse 14, Jesus, after his crucifixion and resurrection from the grave, said he wanted to meet with his disciples that he had been training and tutoring in his ministry, "Afterward he appeared unto the eleven as they sat at meat, and upbraided them with their unbelief and hardness of heart, because they believed not them which had seen him after he was risen." He was talking to his select disciples, when he said to them, "Go ye into all the world, and preach the gospel to every creature. He that believeth and is baptized shall be saved; but he that believeth not shall be damned." Then he began to give the evidences that would follow them that believe. Here's what it says in verse 17, "And these signs" — or these evidences — "shall follow them that BELIEVE."

The question in front of us is the "unbelievers" and the "believers." "He that believeth and is baptized shall be saved; but he that believeth not shall be damned," — the evidences that shall follow the BELIEVER. I hope you have the ability to exercise your intelligence to try to unshackle yourself from denominational prejudices or backgrounds that will describe believers in any other way than what the Bible says. It merely says he that BELIEVES the good news of the gospel and is baptized shall be saved, and he that believes not shall be damned.

Those who believe the good news of the gospel and are baptized and become the saved people shall have the following evidences following their believing . . . "In my name shall they cast out devils." This is where a lot of the controversy regarding the "Charismatic Renewal" hinges. Should these evidences or these emphases be within the framework of the Christian church today? He says, "believers." He doesn't say just the believers of the days of the disciples! He doesn't say that it was just for that generation. If we're going to believe that we can preach the gospel today that he that believeth and is baptized is saved, then we must put those believers in the same category with those believers that we're talking about in the gospel of Mark, chapter 16. We must not separate them by generation or by certain periods of time when they lived or existed. So we have to conclude that if we were reading this in the way that Jesus fully intended it, he was saying, "Even in 1975 he that believeth and is baptized shall be saved, and in 1975 these signs shall follow them that believe. They shall cast out devils, and they shall speak with new tongues." Now, hold onto this, because this is what Mr. Webster says is part of the "charisma" or the "charismatic." IT IS PART OF THE GIFTS. Mr. Webster says this in his own perhaps limited understanding. Jesus said, two of the evidences of the believer will be that they shall cast out devils in my name, and secondly they shall speak with new tongues. It goes on to say that "if they drink any deadly thing," (and I've always put the word "accidentally," because this is not to test or try God) "it shall not hurt them; they shall lay hands on the sick, and they shall recover." This is bringing healing or the helps of healing or the gift of healing that belong to the church. So Jesus spoke concerning these helps.

Sometimes I think the reason people misunderstand the Charismatic Renewal is because we are confused between the old-line Pentecostal concepts and the present-day outpouring of God's Spirit. I think some people who are antagonistic toward the Charismatic Renewal are actually going back a few years and picking up some of the things that were not understood in the era of the Pentecostal outpouring. I know that some of you are asking the question, "Is there any difference between Pentecostalism and the Charismatic Renewal?" I think there definitely is a difference between these two. I hear a lot of Pentecostals say, "Well, I'm Charismatic." They're not Charismatic; they're Pentecostal. I see a vast difference! I was reared Pentecostal, but today I'm deeply involved in the Charismatic Renewal. I can see a lot of differences between the two.

First of all, let me describe one of the differences. Pentecostalism seemingly taught that the baptism of the Holy Spirit and ultimately and subsequently the gifts of the Spirit was a merit badge to the believer. If you had come into this experience, if you tarried long enough, emptied out enough, got rid of all the problems that you could, finally God looked down and said, "Hey, you're a pretty good Joe. You've quit drinking. You've quit going to shows. You've quit smoking. You've quit dancing." We had a whole lot of things we Pentecostals did that we felt God was very offended about, so we said, "Now, you have to get rid of these things, because God is not going to come in and fill a vessel that has all these things in it." We didn't talk much about gossiping or backbiting or jealousy or a lot of things, but we had some external things we knew God wanted everybody to get rid of. So we said, "Now, if you will do your best to get over these things, commit them to God, THEN God will fill you with the baptism of the Holy Spirit." So people were filled with the Holy Spirit, and they felt so great because they had received the merit badge. God had put a stamp on them, "You have really come a long ways now, and I'm going to give you the baptism with the Holy Spirit!"

In the Charismatic Renewal, we understand the opposite to that, that God the Holy Spirit does not wait for you to clean up yourself and do everything yourself. If you can do that, then you don't need the Holy Spirit. IF YOU CAN GET RID OF ALL OF YOUR HANGUPS AND YOUR PROBLEMS AND YOUR SIN AND ALL THESE THINGS, THEN YOU DON'T NEED THE HOLY SPIRIT. The Holy Spirit in the Charismatic Renewal is God's gift to you of his power, his enablement, to help you rise to become what he ultimately wants you to become. This gives a lot of problems to the Pentecostals because they say, "How can a Catholic priest who still prays to Mary speak in tongues?" You see, their concept is that until you quit praying to Mary, the Holy Ghost isn't going to come in. He's waiting for you to do all you can. Then you'll get the merit badge, the baptism with the Holy Ghost and the speaking in other tongues. It doesn't bother me today in the Charismatic Renewal, because I know if a Catholic comes along to the place where he receives the baptism with the Holy Spirit, God is capable of bringing that person ultimately to his own goal for that person. So, it is a God-given power to achieve and accomplish the will and the purposes of God.

That's just one example of the difference between Pentecostalism and the Charismatic. The baptism of the Holy Spirit and the gifts of the Spirit are not merit badges that say to the other person, "This person is better." A lot of people in the "Charismatic" controversy have the idea that Charismatics think they're better than anybody else. They're quite the opposite. This is my view of the Charismatics. Most Charismatics are very humble and feel very much their need of more of the power of God and don't go around saying, "I have the baptism of the Holy Spirit. I am better than you," or that "God endowed me with the Holy Spirit, so therefore, I am better than you or above you in spiritual attainment." The baptism of the Holy Spirit is very humbling. It brings a person to their consciousness that they are nothing. The Holy Spirit comes into a man's or a woman's life to help them become what God wants them ultimately to become.

Another one of the questions in the controversy is, "Doesn't the person receive the Holy Spirit when they are born again?" The Charismatics believe that when a person is born again, they are born again scripturally by the WORKING of the Holy Spirit. There is no way to be born into the family of God without the working of the Holy Spirit, any more than Jesus was born any other way than by the Holy Spirit. Mary the Virgin conceived and bore a child by the Holy Spirit. That's what the Bible says. In other words, Jesus was born of the Holy Spirit. If you are a believer in the church today, regardless of what denominational tag you wear, your new birth, your new life, came only through the working of the Holy Spirit bringing you to Jesus Christ and his life into you. Whether or not you've ever been baptized WITH the Holy Spirit, you are born again BY the Holy Spirit! If you have never spoken in other tongues, you're born again and belong to the family of God.

Charismatics do not believe that the baptism with the Holy Spirit and speaking in tongues is salvation. There is a segment of Pentecostals who will tell you that you are not born again until you have spoken in other tongues. There is nothing to give foundation to that kind of thought. Speaking in tongues is not synonymous with salvation. Receiving the baptism of the Holy Spirit is not one and the same with salvation. Jesus was born of the Holy Spirit, but when he came of the age when God was ready for him to be thrust into the ministry, he presented himself to John for baptism in the Jordan River. "And Jesus, when he was baptized, went up straightway out of the water: and, lo, the heavens were opened unto him, and he saw the Spirit of God descending like a dove, and lighting upon him:

and lo a voice from heaven, saying, This is my beloved Son, in whom I am well pleased." Matthew 3:16-17 (KJV)

Jesus had more than one encounter with the Holy Spirit. His birth was by the Holy Spirit, and I conclude that for every born again believer, your new birth was by the same Holy Spirit that Jesus was conceived of when he was born of Mary.

Will you analyze with me for a moment the difference in Jesus before John's baptism and the coming of the dove, and Jesus afterwards? If you will look very carefully you will probably conclude that from the time of the birth of Jesus to his baptism we have only a few sketchy accounts of his childhood, his young adolescence, and his young manhood days.

THERE IS NO ACCOUNT THAT HE WAS A MIRACLE WORKER.

THERE IS NO ACCOUNT THAT HE EVER HEALED.

THERE IS NO ACCOUNT THAT HE WAS SUPER IN ANY WAY.

The only account was when he was twelve years of age when he was with the doctors in Jerusalem. Outside of that account, there is nothing that describes him as a miracle worker or a powerful person, but when he came to John's baptism and the Spirit of God came down upon him and he was led by the Spirit into the wilderness, then it says that he returned "IN THE POWER OF THE SPIRIT."

FROM THAT MOMENT ON HE PERFORMED MIRACLES.

HE TURNED THE WATER INTO WINE.

HE HEALED THE SICK.

HE HEALED THE BLIND, THE LAME, THE LEPERS, THE WOMAN WITH THE ISSUE OF BLOOD, JAIRUS' DAUGHTER, PETER'S MOTHER-IN-LAW!

JESUS HEALED EVERYWHERE HE WENT FROM THE TIME OF HIS ENDUEMENT IN THE SECOND STAGE OF THE POWER OF THE HOLY SPIRIT.

The Charismatics do not believe that the baptism of the Holy Ghost is synonymous with the Holy Spirit. We believe that the baptism of the Holy Spirit is a similar experience to that of Jesus. He had a SECOND encounter with the Holy Ghost. It's an encounter of being filled with the power. Jesus was showing himself again to his disciples in John 20:21-22 (KJV), when he said, "Peace be unto you: as my Father hath sent me, even so send I you. And when he had said this, he breathed on them, and saith unto them, Receive ye the Holy Ghost:" Some people say that this means then that if they received the Holy Ghost, this is the same baptism that is recorded on the Day of Pentecost; but when you read carefully you will discover that the Bible says in John 7:39 (KJV), " . . . for the Holy Ghost was not yet given; because that Jesus was not yet glorified." It is my belief that in John 20:22 these were the first people to be born again, who received the breathing of the Spirit to become born-again believers. Up to this time, they were disciples. They were followers of Jesus. There is a difference in being a disciple and a follower and in being born again. These disciples followed Jesus. They heard his teaching. They were with him. But on this occasion I believe these people were born again. I believe these were the first born-again people of the New Testament. He breathed on them, and said, "Receive ye the Holy Ghost." To this same group of people now, he says in the book of Acts, chapter one and verse four, "Being assembled together with them, commanded them that they should not . . . " Who are these? THE SAME PEOPLE HE BREATHED ON AND SAID, "RECEIVE YE THE HOLY GHOST," . . . commanded them that they should not "depart from Jerusalem, but wait for the promise of the Father, which, saith he, ye have heard of me." Then in verse 8 he says, "But YE SHALL RECEIVE POWER, after that the Holy Ghost is come upon you: and ye shall be witnesses unto me both in Jerusalem, and in all Judaea and in

Samaria, and unto the uttermost part of the earth." I believe that Jesus was talking about two different experiences:

FIRST OF ALL THE NEW BIRTH, BEING BORN AGAIN, COMING INTO SPIRITUAL LIFE THROUGH THE HOLY SPIRIT:

AND SECONDLY, RECEIVING AN ENDUEMENT OF POWER THROUGH THE BAPTISM OF THE HOLY SPIRIT to become the effective witness that God wanted the Church to be.

I would be foolish to tell you that the church through all the centuries was not effective or has not been effective nor that a born-again believer cannot be effective without the baptism of the Holy Spirit. I've known a lot of Christian people genuinely born again who were very effective in their witness, who were very much attuned to God, and were effective in their walk with God. But for some reason or another, Jesus said to his disciples, "Don't go out into the battlefield. Don't leave Jerusalem until you receive the enduement of power."

I see myself as a Christian soldier. I've just been called by my country to enlist for a battle in Viet Nam. My officers have called me in and said, "Now, we've got a battle over there to fight, and we feel that you ought to have some ammunition. We'd hate for you to get out there on the front line without a gun, without some rations on you. We've going to give you all the protection we can with tanks and with airplanes and other things, but we'd like for you to carry along a little rifle. It might come in handy. So, we're going to give you some of these supplies." Let me tell you, if I'm going out to face a literal enemy that's got a rifle that he's aiming at me, and he's got some tanks on the other side and he's got a government behind him, I'm going to want something in my hands, too. This is exactly what Jesus is saying. He didn't say, "Hey, I'm going to make you some kind of an outstanding soldier, and you're going to stand around with a rifle in your hand. You're going to have C rations, and you're going to be somebody." Not at all! He said, I'm going to endue you with power from on high, because you're going to face an enemy that's well-equipped to destroy you unless you have the ammunition that is necessary. The church is not fighting an intellectual battle with just other people out in the world on the intellectual level. We're not trying to fight some kind of a battle in the financial world. I tell you, we're fighting according to the Apostle Paul, a battle that is not against flesh and blood but is against principalities and powers and dominions and kingdoms of darkness. We are involved in a real battle, and God said the only way that battle can ever be fought is for you to receive the enduement of my power so that you can go against the power of your enemy and you can be successful.

The Charismatic Renewal and the people involved in it have no reason to stand back and boast. All we have is the ammunition God has given to us to fight a good fight and to war a good warfare against your enemy and mine that attacks us in a spiritual battle! It's God's enablement for us to fight a successful battle at this very moment!

Beloved, the church is in a battle. I believe that the Charismatic Renewal is God's last spiritual awakening to the world. I don't get up in a lot of pride to say that I'm in the Charismatic Renewal. I see what God is doing today. God is trying to thrust people from all walks of life into a spiritual warfare. If you're thinking the baptism of the Holy Ghost is an insurance policy that makes you have a lot more security and makes you feel a lot better, you've got another thought coming! If you've had problems before you received the baptism with the Holy Spirit, you wait until you get it! You'll have attacks from the devil you've never had before. Many times people who have been filled with the Holy Spirit just couldn't wait to run and tell their pastor! What a shock to have him look down at them as if they were some kind of "quirk" people and ultimately be shown the door. People can't understand, "Why in the world? Here's something that's so wonderful and so beautiful, and yet all of a sudden I'm an outcast."

The baptism of the Holy Spirit is not some sort of a shelter you get in from the battle. It's giving you a gun and putting something in you that says, "I'm going to go out and fight the devil wherever he is." Pretty soon you find yourself in the middle of a big battle, and you say, "What in the world did I do to get into this?"

I grew up as a Pentecostal with my hankie being waved and singing, "Hold the fort, for I am coming." It described us sitting inside the fort with our flags, and we were saying, "Don't worry, Lord. We're going to hold the fort!" But the Charismatics have learned that being filled with the Holy Spirit is not holding the fort. It's getting out of a fort and charging against the devil everywhere he is, even if it's the boss on the job, even if it's the secretary, if it's the school teacher, if it's the kids, whoever. When a person becomes dynamically filled with the Holy Spirit, it thrusts him out of any kind of a fort and puts him right out on the battlefield. This is what is so beautiful about the Charismatic Renewal. Week after week, people come walking in with somebody that they met out on the battlefield, and say, "Here's a capture. We met out on the battlefield, and God has saved him."

The Charismatic Renewal, as I've said, is not merit badges. It's not something that puts us into some sort of a special, unique, super club. What I see as a Charismatic Renewal is a return to what the book of Acts describes as the norm of the New Testament Church. I see the New Testament Church as a group of people much like what I have seen in the Charismatic Renewal.

Let me say this about the Charismatic Renewal. Not everywhere you go are you going to find the same kind of group of people that fly that flag, and I would be foolish to tell you that there is not some error in the Charismatic Renewal. But you can't classify all charismatic groups by something that you have seen that you didn't understand any more than you can classify all Baptists or all Methodists as being the same. There are differences of operations and differences of opinions in different groups. I'm talking from what I have seen in the Charismatic Renewal here and the other areas in which I've been privileged to speak and minister to in different parts of the country and world, but the Charismatic Renewal as I see it today is a group of people who are seeking to come back to the simplicity of the early church, the New Testament church!

For example, in Ephesians 5:18 it says, "And be not drunk with wine, wherein is excess; but be" (and that's an ACTIVE verb — be, being) "filled with the Spirit;" Then it goes on to describe how you ventilate this outpouring of the Holy Spirit or this being filled with the Spirit, and he says that we do that by "Speaking to yourselves in psalms and hymns and spiritual songs, singing and making melody in your heart to the Lord;" That sounds just like the Charismatics I've been exposed to, doesn't it to you?

I'll tell you something else that reminds me of Charismatics. Paul said, "Having done all, to stand." Charismatics stand more than anybody in the world!

He tells us that after being filled with the Spirit, the outcropping of it is "speaking to yourselves in psalms and hymns and spiritual songs, singing and making melody in your heart to the Lord; Giving thanks always for all things unto God and the Father in the name of our Lord Jesus Christ;"

Now here's another indictment against the Charismatics that some people have made recently. It's been said that we're preaching another gospel; that Jesus is the gospel. The Holy Spirit should never replace the person of Jesus; and from what I have seen in the Charismatic Renewal, it is the opposite of that. When a person becomes filled with the Holy Spirit and gets involved in the Charismatic Renewal, as we know it today, he starts in singing about Jesus, "He is Lord," "He's the Savior of my Soul," "He Alone is Worthy." I don't hear any song or choruses lifting up the person of the Holy Spirit. It's lifting up Jesus. The people that I have seen being filled with the Holy Spirit are more in love with Jesus than people who are not filled with the Holy Spirit. They love Jesus! Oh, how I love Jesus. Over and over, it's praise to the person of Jesus. That's scriptural. The Bible says (John 16:13 KJV) that "When he, (the Holy Ghost) the Spirit of truth, is come, he will guide you into all truth:" He not only will guide you into all truth, but he will remind you of things that "I" have said, and it's Jesus that's speaking. When the Holy Spirit comes, he will remind you of Jesus and who he is and what he has said. He will glorify Jesus!

So, you see, to be filled with the Holy Spirit brings an enduement of power into your life and brings the third person of the Trinity into your life so that he can make Jesus more alive and more real. The reason we come to the point of praying for the sick and believing in divine healing is because the Holy Spirit reminds us that Jesus came not only to save the soul but to also heal the body. Go over and read in the book of Psalms, the 103rd Psalm, "Bless the Lord, O my soul, and forget not all his benefits:" He goes on to talk about the iniquities being forgiven and diseases being healed. It's all tied together in the atonement, that is, the forgiveness of sin and the healing of the body. The person becomes filled with the Holy Spirit, and the Holy Spirit begins to make Jesus alive. Then, we become conscious of the fact that he wants to heal us of our physical and emotional problems as well as to forgive us and cleanse us from our sin sickness.

So, the Holy Spirit as I see it today is not creating a people who are on a super-ego trip that think they're somebody. They are a people who submit themselves one to another in the love and in the fear of God, believing what God's word says, that he would endow us with power and give unto us the helps so that we would be able to be strengthened, to be edified, to be comforted, and to be uplifted as a group of people within the body of Christ.

Charismatics are not negative against anybody. They're not against any denomination. Charismatics love people they do not understand. Charismatics are not out to start a new denomination. Martin Luther wasn't trying to start a new denomination. All he wanted was for new life to come back into the Roman Catholic Church. John Knox did not intend to start the Presbyterian. He just wanted God's life to be in the church. John and Charles Wesley did not intend to start the Methodist Church. They wanted life in the church. God is going to have a people, call that people whatever you may. The Charismatics today are not interested in starting a new denomination. In fact, most Charismatics would just love to see their own church come alive in the Holy Spirit and worship God and love God, and they would like to stay right with their own denomination.

One of the questions I've been most often asked in the Charismatic Renewal is, "Should I stay in my church, or should I leave?" I'm going to tell you, even with my Pentecostal background, what I tell them. Stay as long as you can. As long as you can breathe, stay there; but if you get where you can't breathe, you have no alternative. You've got to find a place where you can breathe spiritually and stay alive. I want you to know that's not just something I say because I think I ought to say it. There's nothing that would thrill this pastor's heart more than for the church down the street with a different flag to have the same moving of God I see in the Bible and as I see it in the Charismatic Renewal. It would thrill my heart for Houston to come alive, and I don't care what name is over the church. But, I want to see God's people come into that beautiful position of being endued with the power from on high, bringing healing to humanity that is sick in mind, body, and in spirit and to see the church come alive to welcome the glorious return of our Lord and Savior Jesus Christ in the clouds of Glory.

As a Pentecostal, I think there were times that I did not really have a desire to see my denominational friends have an experience as I could see in the Bible. I think I almost felt that they were condemned; and I didn't have any real love or compassion when God touched my life anew after having pastored for many years and done the best that I knew how to do. I'll not forget the moment nor the time nor the year that God touched my life afresh. Almost in one split second of time, when I saw God in a complete new way, I saw myself in another way, I saw the Church in a new way, I saw the Bible in a new way, I saw the world in a new way. My Bible was almost completely re-written. Let me tell you, it's as difficult as a Pentecostal to get in the Charismatic Renewal and in the move of God as it is for a Baptist or a Catholic or a Presbyterian or anyone else. It may be more difficult. I don't have anything to go by, but I sometimes think that it is more difficult, because we Pentecostals have had a move of God and we have been acquainted with the gifts of the Spirit and these things. Because of that, I think we had some hangups that made it more difficult; but I remember the time when God was touching men like Jim Brown, the Presbyterian; Dennis Bennett, the Episcopalian; Father McNutt and others that are of other denominations. I didn't ask for God to touch my life anew. I wouldn't have known what to ask God for anyway. I would have probably concluded that I already knew, but God in his infinite grace touched my life and everything began to happen and began to change. I began to go through deaths. I got into some battles that I did not know how to get out of, and one of the difficulties in this moment is that what God is doing he is doing so quickly that there are no books that can be published in the next battle and in the next decision.

It's like a pilgrim walking through a jungle. You come to rivers, you come to mountains that have never been charted. The underbrush of the jungle is so dense that there is no way to see beyond the step tomorrow. The faithfulness of the Holy Spirit is right there to hack through the jungle, to forge the rivers, to climb the mountains, and to move on.

Charismatics have not arrived. They are on the march. They don't know it all, but they're learning! The Bible says, "Now I would not have you ignorant, brethren . . ." Charismatics are studying to know what God's will is today for their lives!

SHIRLEY NORWOOD

"I had really lost interest in reading the Bible. I thought miracles had stopped a long time ago, and if anyone was ever healed, WE WERE SHOCKED! The only regret I have is that I didn't accept the baptism ten years ago when this happened in our church back home in Kansas City."

"Don't store up treasures here on earth where they can erode away or may be stolen. Store them in heaven where they will never lose their value, and are safe from thieves. If your profits are in heaven your heart will be there too." Matt. 6:19-21 (TLB)

Shirley doesn't appear to even be thinking of her riches as she efficiently pours her time and energy into work for which she receives no earthly pay. Praise God for her husband, Jim, for providing their earthly needs — willingly as she spends much time in work for Jesus. Surely they have a LARGE heavenly bank account. She does receive compensation while she works as a consultant for Mary Kay Cosmetics.

We see her energetically, voluntarily working at Hunter Ministries office almost every time we are there. She is also our make-up artist for television production.

She has taught in church schools since she was 18.

She has been pre-school director for her church. She has served on practically every board and committee in her church. She has been conference leader in several places, teaching teachers. She and her husband are counselors on the 700 Club.

We love to be around her because of her charisma, sharing Jesus from the depths of her devoted, energetic heart.

Would you like to get excited?
READ and BE!

Why should "I" speak in tongues? Wow! For almost three years I was feeling a real dullness in my Christian life. It wasn't because I wasn't going to church, because I was there practically every time the doors opened, Sunday morning and night and Wednesday and whenever else there was a meeting of some kind that needed to be attended. I kept telling my husband, "Jim, there's something missing in my life." He kept saying, "I'm completely satisfied. You're not, because you're not teaching eleven and twelve year olds like you used to. You've been at pre-school work just too long." I said, "No, that's not it." I HAD REALLY LOST INTEREST IN READING THE BIBLE. It just didn't mean anything when I read it, IF I got around to it.

I was raised a Baptist, and my parents were faithful in taking me to church when I was young. I accepted Christ as my personal Savior when I was eleven years old, and when I was eighteen I began teaching girls eleven and twelve years old and was constantly busy being in church. After I married I started directing the children's choir. I was right in there doing everything you can imagine a young person can do in a church, full steam ahead. When our daughter Kim was born I started attending pre-school conferences and became very interested in how little children from birth through age three can be taught about Jesus and his love for them. So for the past twelve years I've been in pre-school work in our church, leading conferences in the state and in other churches, teaching teachers how they can teach the young children.

My life still wasn't exciting spiritually. In January of 1973, during our Training Union time, it was announced in the bulletins that we were going to have an author, Frances Hunter, as a guest speaker. I had heard some of the others say how much they had enjoyed her books, but I had never gotten around to reading them. I had at one time loved to read, but that too had gotten away from me.

I went. Oh, the things she said, the things she told... I sat there and I cried, I laughed, I got so excited hearing her give her testimony about her love for Jesus!

Time was passing, months went by, and I still felt this void in my life. May 10, 1973, our Sunday School Department was having a ladies luncheon in our department director's home. I really had gotten to the point I didn't enjoy going to class meetings, because we'd eat and then it was just gab, gab, gab! Then, they'd have a quick devotion, and that was all. I heard Frances was going to be there and because I had enjoyed her so much, I decided I would go.

Frances was going to speak first. Then we were going to have a luncheon. I had to leave early for my daughter's orthodontist appointment.

Frances spoke on how to make Jesus come alive in your life through reading the Bible. We really got a lot out of the talk. Then, at the very end, she even had an invitation! That kind of shocked me, because I thought, "Here we are in a Baptist Sunday School group, and she's giving an invitation!" Then, she said, "I have two or three minutes left. Would you like to know what is going on in the world today?" Of course, all of us, about thirty of us, were eager. We all said, "Yes, we want to know!" So, Frances started telling about how God had told them to have a miracle service on a Tuesday night in a Baptist Church in El Paso, Texas, and how word got to the schools that Jesus was going to be passing by the church and healing the sick, the maimed, and the lame. A little child with cerebral palsy heard the good news and begged and pleaded to go until she finally got someone to take her. Frances said she was healed, fell under the power, and started speaking in tongues. When she said this I started having a million questions, because I knew that my Bible said that you are not to speak in tongues unless you have an interpretation, and she had said nothing about anybody interpreting what that girl had said. I also was very interested in this, because I had been out canvassing our neighborhood just before that to collect *cerebral palsy* donations.

She said a lot of things within that few minute period. She told how she had been to a Kathryn Kuhlman miracle service and how she had fallen under the power. Then she quickly closed!

I had hundreds of questions running through my mind that needed answers. Just then a friend came up and asked Frances if she would pray for someone who was very sick. Frances said, "Let's all stop and pray for this friend of Betty Jo's." We all closed our eyes, and Frances prayed. I heard a little bit of a commotion and thought, "Oh, I guess everybody is getting ready to hold hands." I opened my eyes to get someone's hand, and BETTY JO WAS NOT STANDING UP ANYMORE. SHE WAS LYING ON THE FLOOR! All of our mouths were gaping open! I can remember someone bending over Betty Jo and wondering what to do. Frances just laughed and said, "Leave her alone. She is with Jesus, and she'll never be any happier than she is right now." I thought, "What is this woman talking about?" Betty Jo got up and was smiling. It seemed as if everyone else wanted to ignore the whole thing!

Someone called dinner time, and I thought, "I want to know if Betty Jo knew she was falling on the floor." I wanted to know! I went all through the house trying to find Betty Jo to ask her the questions that were in my mind. I finally found her and said, "I've got some questions to ask you." I was shaking all over! I didn't realize that this was the power of the Holy Spirit that had fallen upon me during Frances' prayer. Betty Jo said, "Sure! Let's go in the other bedroom." So we did, and I asked her as many questions as I could. It was already past the time for that orthodontist appointment I was to have left for. I hadn't even picked Rhonda (my daughter) up, and I was on the other side of town. However, I asked as many questions as

I could and left quickly, shaking all the way to pick up Rhonda at school, saying, "Lord, what is this? Show me. I don't understand." All I wanted to do really was to go home and read my Bible. Yet I couldn't. I had to take my daughter to the orthodontist!

A couple of weeks later I went to deliver some cosmetics to a friend who had just moved back into town. She was a member of the First Baptist Church. I started telling her what had happened at our class meeting. She said, "WOW! You mean this happened, and you didn't invite me to the luncheon!" I said, "I didn't know it was going to happen." I mentioned Kathryn Kuhlman, and she said, "I think I read somewhere that Kathryn Kuhlman is going to be in town." I said, "Well, if you hear of this, let me know, because I want to go."

I started piecing things together and remembered about a year ago some girls in my Sunday School class had talked about getting on a bus and going to a Kathryn Kuhlman service. The Lord had brought this back to my memory, but I remembered just a little bit of it. I started calling different ones and said, "Is there going to be a bus this year?" They didn't know anything about it. They were really hesitant to tell me who had even ordered that bus. I said, "Why are you keeping it a secret?" They said, "Because not everybody believes this." I said, "Please keep checking, and if there is a bus please let me know."

My mother had gotten really sick, had a temperature of 106° and was put in the hospital. Not knowing what was wrong with her, the doctors had put her in isolation and were giving her all kinds of tests. I kept wanting to go help her, but she said, "No, there's nothing you can do now. Don't come until they let me out of the hospital." I kept waiting and told the people that I would call, "Please keep checking about the bus to the Kathryn Kuhlman service, and if you find out anything, call my husband and let him know. I'm going to have to go to Kansas City to be with my mother."

Right after Frances had been to the luncheon I had written Mother all about what had happened at the Sunday School luncheon. When I finally arrived in Kansas City, Mother said, "There is something missing in my life. If God doesn't do something about it, I don't know what I'm going to do!" I took care of my mother and told her, "I have to leave on Saturday, because Kathryn Kuhlman is going to be in Houston on Sunday." I had been with my mother almost two weeks. My husband had called and told me about the meeting. I had asked him to see if he could get me a ticket to go on a bus, thus reserving a seat, so I'd know for sure I could get in.

I got home about midnight and was so tired from my trip that I stayed home the next day, Sunday, and slept. We NEVER miss church on Sunday, but God was in control! At ten o'clock that morning the phone rang. The lady said, "I'm Betty from your church." I was still sleepy, but I knew that she was the lady who worked in the library. She said, "I understand you want to go to the Kathryn Kuhlman service. I have an extra ticket for the bus. Would you like to have it?"

I went to Evangelistic Temple where we were to catch the bus and arrived just as the services were being dismissed. I heard someone mention "AGLOW" in passing and wondered what that was. Someone introduced me to Wanda, who was a Baptist but was coming out of Evangelistic Temple. I thought, "I wonder what a Baptist is doing there?" She gave me a big old bear hug as if she had known me all her life, and that was really the first time I'd ever met her.

At the meeting we sat right above the wheel chair section in the audience. All I could do that whole time was pray for all those people. I thought when Kathryn prayed for these people and they fell, they were receiving the Holy Spirit. I thought that was how you received the Holy

Spirit. I was inspired! So many things were whirling around in my mind.

We had to get back to church, because our choir was doing a special number. Yet I did not want to go again. The thing I wanted to do was to get into the Bible. Instead, I went to church but did not enjoy it. All I could think about was reading the Bible.

I called Betty and asked what she had been able to see at the Kathryn Kuhlman meeting, since she sat in the choir. Betty answered only what I asked. Because of my inquisitiveness, she kept telling a little bit more and a little bit more. Later I'd think of another question and call her back. She'd tell me a little more. This happened again and again!!

I wrote to Mother and told her that I now knew what she was missing. Betty had given me some books to read, A NEW SONG and THE TWO SIDES OF A COIN.

We left on our vacation on June 30th to South Dakota to go camping with my parents. On July 1st as we came out of the motel room I noticed something on the trailer that I had never noticed before. It said, "In case of emergency call such and such a number." It gave me a funny feeling! That day while traveling a young boy pulled out in a pickup truck and we could not stop. Jim said, "Shirley, we're going to hit him." I had been reading at that time about Shirley Boone receiving the baptism in the Holy Spirit. I looked up, and we were heading right toward the truck. At the very last minute, Jim turned the wheel or God did. Our car only sideswiped him. Jim was knocked unconscious. Blood was streaming from him. I thought the car was going around and around in circles, and I kept waiting for it to stop, not realizing until that night when I thought back upon it that the car had stopped straight on the road. I had been hit on the back of the head by the steering wheel or something, and a great big knot was there. My daughters had been asleep. We all had severe concussions. My husband had a fractured skull and elbow. I had a sprung tailbone. My teeth were knocked out of line by the impact.

I said, "Start praying, Kim. Start praying." The Lord was with us all through this time. Jim became semiconscious. He did not know where he was and could not make any sense when he talked. We were taken to a twelve-bed hospital, and we had four of the beds! I went over and laid hands on my husband and said, "Lord, just heal him." Betty had shared a little about this with me, but I had not received the baptism of the Holy Spirit at that time.

For a whole month, we were off work, and the Lord had us listening to tapes which Betty shared. We read books. I was consuming the Bible! GOD HAD MADE THE WORD COME ALIVE. I kept saying, "Lord, when did you put that in there?" I had read the Bible all my life, but now it became so alive! I just couldn't believe what was popping out of those scriptures! I'd get up early in the morning and would read all day long; God's word or books that Betty was feeding me, or I would listen to tapes. IT WAS EXCITING!

August 21st came, the day of the first Hunter meeting I would be able to attend. I kept saying to Betty, "Why am I not seeing these miracles?" She kept saying, "Shirley, you won't see them at the Baptist Church, because they believe that these things stopped years ago." I knew this, because we had been talking about it, that these things had passed, even though we prayed that someone would be healed if it would be God's will. However, IF THEY EVER GOT HEALED WE WERE SHOCKED.

I just knew I was going to receive the baptism in the Holy Spirit at the meeting that night. A friend from another Baptist church went with me. We sat on the very front row. All of a sudden Charles started calling out healings. One was arthritis, and right on the front row a lady let out a scream and said, "My legs! My legs!" Charles said, "Come on up on the stage and tell us what God has done." They had to help her up on the stage. She seemed drunk. She said, "God has just healed me of gout and arthritis." I thought, "My mother has gout." Just as she said this, down she fell. They hadn't even touched her. I was so excited, because when she got back up she said, "I'm a Baptist."

Frances then called for all the pastors to come up so that she could ask Jesus to bless them that they might be renewed in their faith and their strength to minister to their people. Then, after she did that she said, "I want everyone to come up who is a Sunday School teacher." My husband and Glenda jumped up to go forward, and they said, "Come on, Shirley." I said, "I can't. I'm not an actual teacher now." I was a substitute teacher. I was still in the pre-school area working as a hostess. When they needed a teacher I would teach, but I was not an actual voted-in Sunday School teacher that year. So I couldn't go, I thought. Then, all of a sudden she said, "Anybody who works in Sunday School, come on up." I went up. She prayed for my husband, and down he went. I gave a little laugh, and she said, "Was that your husband?" I said, "Yes." She said, "Well, let me pray for you, too. When I pray for you I'm going to ask them to join your hands." She prayed, and down I went! They joined our hands. Then she prayed that the Lord would bless our marriage. "I've received?" Again when I got up my husband said, "Shirley, you were down a long time." I said, "Jim, did I really receive?" He said, "You were sure saying something that I didn't understand."

I watched Glenda, my friend. She was up on that stage, and I knew that she had received. I had seen her fall. Then, here she came with all of her doubts and everything saying, "They pushed me." I said, "No, they didn't. I was watching." I said, "You did receive."

She talked about her knee having problems. She said,

"My husband is home tonight doing housework that I cannot do, because I cannot get down on my knees." I hadn't realized that. I said, "Go on up there and have them pray for you." She said, "I'm not going back up there." I said, "Yes! We'll go to Frances and ask her to pray for your knee! God will heal it!" You see, I'd been reading all these books, and Glenda hadn't. My faith was great! Jim said, "I'll go with you." So, we went up there, and I told Frances what the problem was. Frances just said, "Jesus heal it." She touched Glenda, and down she went! Then, up she popped again and said, "Did she push me?" She said, "Oh! My knee! I was so concerned about whether she pushed me or not that I didn't notice that my knee is healed!" An usher was standing there and said, "Yes, awhile ago when you got up I had to help you; but this time you jumped right up." She was so excited about her knee. Then, I was back up again asking Frances to pray for my neighbor who couldn't come. Instead, she asked the Lord to anoint my hands to pray for my neighbor, to ask that Jesus would heal his kidneys. I kept thinking, "Lord, he's only got one kidney." Down I went again! That was three times in one night! But it was exciting to see what the Lord had done.

I had sent my mother some tapes to listen to. She called and said, "Shirley, are you all right? You have constantly been on my mind. Are you sure everything is all right?" I said, "Yes." She was so concerned while we were talking and later told me that she had really thought I was having an affair. I told her, "I was but it was with JESUS!"

On September 1st we went to our first Full Gospel Business Men's meeting. I bought nine books, all books I had already read; but I wanted Mother to read them, too. Then, I saw one more book, ANGELS OF LIGHT. We had already written the check, but I asked Jim if we could buy this. He didn't want to write another check, but he said, "If it costs less than $1.00 I'll let you have it." It cost $.95.

Praise the Lord!

By listening to a cassette tape we found out how Christians can be oppressed by demons. MAN, WAS THAT A SHOCK! I knew my husband had been reading some Edgar Cayce books. I had been saying to him that I didn't believe in this. I thought it was fairy tale stuff. I did not realize the power that Satan has with such things as horoscopes, e.s.p., transcendental meditation, yoga, etc. I just thought it was foolishness, so I did not get myself involved. I knew my husband loved to read books by such people as Jeanne Dixon and Edgar Cayce. I said, "Jim, I'm getting so concerned. You're reading these books much more than you are the Bible. If you read something so much you are going to believe it instead of what God's word says."

In reading ANGELS OF LIGHT, I saw how these things were not of God. I talked to a friend about it. I know now how much the Lord let her be in my life, because when I needed an answer the phone was always available. Now if I want to call up to ask her a question of non-importance, her line is never free, because she counsels so much. She said she knew of someone who prayed for deliverance. She said, "Shirley, don't spread this to too many people, because even some Charismatics do not believe that Christians can be oppressed by demons." I thought, "Wow! They need to read this book."

I talked my husband into going. On September 6th we went over for deliverance. My husband had healings, and we got to see legs grow out, which was exciting!

When this started happening to me there were three people that I wanted to share with. They were my mother, my uncle, and a girl in Kansas City who had multiple sclerosis. Little did I know until I went home at Christmas time that the Lord had already healed her of multiple sclerosis and that she had already received the Holy Spirit a long time ago.

My mother told me that my uncle was going to come up Thanksgiving to talk to me about all of this, because he was very concerned. Among the tapes I had sent to my mother was one of Jerry Horner, who was Professor of Greek and New Testament and Chairman of the Theology Department at tte Baptist college in Missouri where my uncle had been counselor and dean of men. My uncle was now a Southern Baptist preacher. When I got word of this, I was really excited! I started laughing and praising the Lord. I thought, what is wrong with me? My Uncle Johnny is going to come and really get all over me, because he thinks this is not of the Lord. And, I'm excited!!

I immediately called Betty and asked her to pray for a miracle! We prayed that God would perform a miracle that weekend. God started working, and it was exciting how he started working! I didn't even know what was going to be happening during that time. I wondered what I could take them to.

On the 15th of September, Betty had invited us to a prayer meeting at her home. Just before we were to go, my older daughter, Rhonda, went to lie down. I discovered she had 103° temperature. I called Ed and said, "Ed, do you believe in miracles? If you do, pray for Rhonda. If we are to come to that prayer meeting, God has got to heal Rhonda."

He prayed with her. We went ahead and ate, and because I had been taught that if your children are sick you keep them home and don't expose them to other people, I stayed home. I said, "Jim, you go, and when Rhonda's temperature gets completely down I'll come." I told Rhonda, "Start praising the Lord." We had just received a letter from Frances telling us about the 700 Club. I asked Rhonda if she would like to watch the 700 Club. We turned it on, and Pat Robertson said if anyone was sick we should put our hands on the television and believe for a miracle. We prayed, and I didn't know anything had happened. We got dressed and got in the car, turning on the Christian radio station. I heard, "If anyone is sick, ask the elders to pray with you, anointing the sick with oil." I said, "Lord, are you trying to tell me something?" When we arrived at the prayer meeting, my husband was lying on the floor! He had just received the baptism in the Holy Spirit. Ed was in tears. He was so happy to see us all. They checked Rhonda. Her temperature was normal. She said, "Mother, do you remember when that man said, 'Somebody has a throat condition and it is being healed?' " Then she said, "My throat stopped hurting." I hadn't even known that it was hurting. It was in just one week's time that the Lord did all this in our family. That night my youngest daughter, Kim, also received the baptism!

My mother had said, "If there is going to be a Hunter meeting, you let me know, because I want to come down and check this all out." On September 20th she came, she saw, and she received the baptism with the Holy Spirit at a Hunter meeting. On the 22nd we were watching the 700 Club, and Pat Robertson had a word of knowledge about someone having a spur in the back being healed. It was Mother's back.

By the time Thanksgiving came, my uncle had already received the baptism over the phone. Instead of "getting all over me," my mother and Uncle Johnny both got to give a little of their testimony that night! The next day we had Ed and Betty come over to share, and my aunt's gall bladder was healed right in our front room! My cousin received the baptism in the Holy Spirit. The next night the Barnwells came over to share, and my daughter Rhonda received the baptism in the Holy Spirit, making our whole family complete in receiving the baptism in the Holy Spirit. It's just been glorious knowing that I can pray to the Lord any time in my prayer language and knowing that our family is complete in this, too. The Lord has shown us many miracles!

Why should "I" speak in tongues? Because my precious Lord has become so real to me. As I grew up I always went to church, always believed in God; I had already trusted him as my Savior. This was a transaction between him and me, a truly beautiful one, where he truly became the lover of my soul. I want to praise God that he has so much patience, so much love, so much grace and mercy, that he cared enough to stick by me, to keep after me, and to make me hungry for his word. The only regret I have is that I didn't accept the baptism ten years ago when this happened in our church back home in Kansas City. Our pastor received and some of the members, but I was too ignorant to understand what was going on. Praise God, he never let me go but showed me the truth on August 21, 1973.

DR. JERRY AND ANN
HORNER
Associate Professor
of Biblical Literature,
Oral Roberts
University.

Jerry: "Before the baptism I could take a passage of scripture and analyze it grammatically, BUT IT DIDN'T BEAT WITH THE PULSE OF THE LIVING GOD IN IT! The baptism of the Holy Spirit brought new areas of spiritual understanding in my life. The Bible is no longer a textbook, it has become a LIVING word to me, but YOU CAN NEVER EXPECT TO HAVE THE BAPTISM OF THE HOLY SPIRIT IF YOU ARE CONTENT TO LIVE WITHOUT IT."

Ann: "I BLAMED MY PASTOR FOR NOT HAVING THE SPIRITUAL GROWTH THAT I LACKED IN MY LIFE. I sat at church Sunday after Sunday, Sunday after Sunday, bored. Now Jesus has become real to me!"

Jerry
BA — Union University, Jackson, Tennessee
BD & M.Div., Th.D. — Southwestern Baptist Theological Seminary, Ft. Worth, Texas
Post Graduate Work at Cambridge University and Manchester University, England.
Listed in Who's Who in American Education

Listed in Who's Who in Religion
Listed in Outstanding Educators of America
Author of Publications: Five Portraits of Christ; An Outline Survey of the New Testament; numerous articles in theological and educational journals.
Frequent speaker at conferences, conventions and seminars in Christian circles. Has traveled in more than 60 countries. Ordained minister. Professor of Greek and New Testament and Chairman of the Division of Christianity and Philosophy at Southwest Baptist College, Bolivar, Missouri, 1962-1973. Associate Professor of Biblical Literature, Oral Roberts University, Tulsa, Oklahoma, 1973-Present. Evangelical Theological Society. Association of Baptist Professors of Religion.

Ann
BA — Southwest Baptist College, Bolivar, Missouri. Majored in Elementary Education. Taught five years — Elementary Education.

"When God began creating the heavens and the earth, the earth was at first a shapeless, chaotic mass, with the Spirit of God brooding over the dark vapors." Gen. 1:1-2(TLB)

". . . He (God's Son) regulates the universe by the mighty power of his command." Heb. 1:3 (TLB)

"He was before all else began and it is his power that holds everything together." Col. 1:17 (TLB)

Jerry, with all his BA, BD & M.Div. & Th.D., his Cambridge University and his Manchester University, found that education, theological knowledge and salvation left his earthly world of religion as a shapeless, chaotic mass (better pronounced mess). He was trying with intellectual determination of the flesh to regulate his spiritual universe by his own might instead of the mighty POWER of "his" command. God's command in Ephesians 5:18 is to "be filled instead with the Holy Spirit, and controlled by him."

THEN HE SPOKE IN TONGUES!!! and now it is "HIS POWER" that holds everything together!

Jerry

It's the greatest, most exciting thing in the world to be a child of God, to enjoy the fullness of God's Holy Spirit! I personally went for years and years and years as a carnal Christian. I have the best education that my denomination can give me. Then I did post-graduate work at Cambridge University in England, and at Manchester University in England. For eleven years I served as professor of Greek and New Testament and as Chairman of the Theology Department in a Southern Baptist college. In all that time there was still a lack in my life. I could take a passage of scripture and analyze it grammatically. BUT IT DIDN'T BEAT WITH THE PULSE OF THE LIVING GOD IN IT. All of these attainments faded into insignificance when the glory of Jesus burst upon me!

I could see where Paul characterized people into three groups. He called one group the natural. They don't have the Spirit of God at all. They are not even Christians. They're perishing. He called one group the carnal. They're children of God. They've been born again, but they've never entered into the fullness of God's Holy Spirit. Then, there was the group that he called the spiritual, the mature, those who have gone on in the Lord, those who have been filled with his Holy Spirit.

Years ago, when I was just a young student pastor at the First Church, I was in the county seat, and here were some soberly dressed women going around taking up a collection right on the street. I was standing on the sidewalk talking with some people who lived in the little community where I was serving as pastor. It so happened that the people to whom I was talking were Pentecostals. This lady came up with her offering box and she said, "Would you like to contribute to help build our church building?"

I said, "What church is it, Ma'am?"

She said, "It's the Church of God."

I fished out a quarter! The lady I was talking with told the woman, "You're getting that from a Baptist Preacher." Brother, did she put on a show! "Praise the Lord!" she said, "Son, keep on praying. You'll see the light. I'm going to pray for you, that the Lord will fill you with the Holy Spirit." She really got to dancing in the Lord. I said later I was glad I didn't put a dollar in the offering plate!

I don't know whether that lady prayed or not. If she did, the Lord finally answered that one!

Several years ago, knowing that something was lacking in my life, I prayed, "Lord, I don't care what you have to do. Just do it! Just do what you've got to do!" That's a dangerous prayer when you leave God wide open like that. He did it . . . Brother he did it!

The Lord had been dealing with me for several years until there came into my life an overpressing burden so heavy upon me that I felt like I literally was in hell. I would agonize before the Lord. I would spend hours flat on my face agonizing before God, weeping bitterly on and on and on. There was no relief.

One thing that kept me going all this time was my firm belief in the faithfulness of God. I believed the word of God to be true, and I believed God meant it when he said that he would not allow us to go through any trial beyond our ability to endure. I knew that God was faithful. That was the one thread that held me up.

Several things happened. I read Corrie Ten Boom's book, THE HIDING PLACE. One thing stayed with me from that book and that was where she and her sister in the German concentration camp praised God for ALL things, even the fleas that infested the barracks. "Praise God for the fleas!" That stayed with me.

When I got as low as I could get, which is just where God wanted me, the Lord was ready! I was able to attend my home church one Sunday evening. I had not been there for months. I had been out visiting other places.

There was a family visiting there from Kansas City, complete strangers to me. After the service this woman came up to me and handed me a book. She said to me, "The Lord has told me to give you this book." I said, "Well, thank you." I looked at the title and said, "Well, maybe this has some answers for me." She said; "Before we left home this afternoon, I felt compelled to put this book in my purse. I didn't know why, but I know the Lord well enough to know that he had some reason for it. The Lord told me during this service to give you this book." The book was Merlin Carother's book PRISON TO PRAISE. I read the book twice that night and felt pretty good the next day. The book spoke to me.

I warn you if any of you are seeking a closer walk with the Lord Jesus Christ and you want to move on with the Lord, the devil is going to be right there with you. When anybody begins to make progress in the Lord, the devil is going to do his worst to try to put a roadblock in the way. So by Tuesday I felt more miserable than ever, because the devil was giving me the full weight of his power. Again I was in agony before God. Right out of the blue the Lord spoke to me and said, "Open the Bible."

"Where?" I've never been one to go to the Bible cafeteria style and just close my eyes and point. I'm afraid of what I might point at. But the impression was so strong: "Open the Bible." So I opened the Bible and the very first word I saw was "praise." Praise God. The living praise God; the dead cannot praise God and so on. I had no idea where it was. I looked up a few lines before that and this statement looked like it was underscored in bright colors. "It was for my welfare that I had great bitterness." "IT WAS FOR MY WELFARE THAT I HAD GREAT BITTERNESS." (RSV)

I saw this was Isaiah chapter 38, King Hezekiah's experience. He was going to die. Later the Lord added to his years, but in the midst of his sorrow he wrote this poem describing the bitterness that he felt, the agony. I said, "Man, this is me." I identified with that. He talked about how he cried out to the Lord day and night. Then he saw the hand of God in this and said, "It was for my welfare that I had great bitterness." This directed me to the twelfth chapter of Hebrews, a passage concerning the Lord's discipline that I had taught and preached for years BUT HAD NEVER EXPERIENCED! It tells how the Lord loves us so much that he brings discipline into our lives as his children to bring us into his holiness. When I read those words the very first thought that came to me was, "God, how you must love me! How you must really love me!" I'll tell you why — because way back months before when I was in such deep agony, the Lord could have delivered me at that moment, and I would have known some measure of peace. But where were the lessons I needed to learn? Where was the spiritual maturity I needed to reach? Where was all of this fullness that God wanted me to have? It took great love for God to restrain himself from reaching down and giving me deliverance at that time. It took great love for God to bring me through all of these trying times and then to lift me up. THINGS BEGAN TO HAPPEN FROM THAT POINT ON.

The next thing of significance that happened after the Lord began dealing with me in this way was in a convention to which I brought a series of Bible studies. The annual sermon at this convention was preached by a young man, one of the most successful Baptist pastors in the State of Missouri and the pastor of one of the largest churches in the state. He announced his sermon topic as "The Dangers of the Charismatic Movement."

I was sitting on the front row. I didn't know anything about the Charismatics. I didn't know anything about the full gospel movement, but one thing I did know was that no man could put a curb on the Spirit of God. No man can shut the Spirit of God up in a cage and say, "You just can't do that today."

This young man said, "Miracles were reserved for the first century." I thought, "He's got his eyes closed. Where has he been?" He said that speaking in tongues is of the devil. He said that the spiritual gifts were meant only for the first century church. I've read the New Testament; I've studied it . . . I've taught it! I'VE NEVER SEEN THAT ANYWHERE. One thing in particular that he said really raised my curiosity. He said, in a ridiculing manner, "Do you know what they're doing now? They're growing legs!" I didn't know what he was talking about! He said, "Yeah, they're getting somebody with one leg shorter than the other, and they're praying that the Lord will lengthen their legs."

People really thought that was funny, but I didn't, because my mother has one leg about five inches shorter than the other. As a young girl she fell and dislocated her hip, and she grew up crippled. It never occurred to me until that precise moment that I could pray for my mother physically. He went on, and my interest was really aroused. He preached a vehement sermon against the Charismatics and against the Spirit of God. The Lord used that sermon mightily, because as I drove home he just bathed me in his word and in his love.

I was praying, "Lord, just fill me to overflowing. Fill me to capacity. Let it overflow, and then enlarge my capacity for more." I began to re-study the word of God. The Lord gave me a hunger and a thirst for his word that I had never known before. When you've got a hungry heart for God, he is going to feed you until you are fed! When you reach out to God he is right there to meet you!

One day as I was driving to Springfield, Missouri, I began to think about spiritual gifts. "Meant for the first century only." No, I didn't believe that. Who in the world would want a God who has lost all of his zip? Could God do one thing in one century but not in another century?

Could God perform the miracle of creation? Could Jesus Christ perform miracles of healing? Could Jesus do all of these wondrous things then but not now? HAS GOD LOST ALL OF HIS POWER? What kind of a God is that? If Jesus doesn't have the same kind of compassion now upon people as he did 2,000 years ago, what's wrong with him? What changed him? I began to see the truth about spiritual gifts and the fullness of God's Holy Spirit.

One thing that always bothered me was a study I did on the "terrible" topic of speaking in tongues several years ago. I presented this at the Missouri Baptist Convention. It was published in booklet form, and thousands of copies have been distributed. I never denied that it was valid for today. I was open to that. I mean, "WE didn't need it. It was for a bunch of spiritual babies and thumb suckers but we really don't have to have this." The thing that really bothered me was that I identified the baptism in the Holy Spirit with conversion. While I was writing that the Lord used a passage of scripture in Acts 1 that gave me a lot of trouble, when Jesus told his apostles, "You shall be baptized with the Holy Spirit in just a few days." Weren't those disciples already Christians? If they were Christians didn't they have the Holy Spirit? You can't be a Christian without the presence of the Holy Spirit, but here Jesus was saying to these men, "You're going to be baptized in the Holy Spirit." That really bothered me. It shook my Baptist upbringing quite a bit. (It needed shaking up.)

On this occasion, while I was driving down the highway, I said, "Now, look. Everything that is a gift of God is of grace. I don't work for it. I don't agonize for it. God doesn't reward me for a bunch of spiritual merits. God doesn't chalk up points in my favor and wait until I've got enough of them to earn a gift! What do we do then to receive a gift? Nothing except we take the hand of faith and reach out and grab the free gift."

How did I get saved? I asked the Lord Jesus Christ to

save me, and I believed that he saved me. I claimed it through faith. How do I get any spiritual gift? I simply ask and receive in faith. On this occasion I said, "Lord Jesus, I pray that you will baptize me in the Holy Spirit and, Lord, I thank you. I believe that you've done it. Lord, I know that speaking in tongues is a manifestation of the baptism in the Holy Spirit. I've been taught that this is the devil but I don't believe that! I WANT EVERYTHING YOU HAVE FOR ME. I'm going to open my mouth to praise you, and I want the Holy Spirit to take complete control." There, alone with the Lord, I opened my mouth. I think I got the word "Lord" out. Then the dam broke. It really broke! It was terrific.

I began thinking, "If this is of the devil, it sure feels good." BUT I KNEW IT WAS OF THE LORD. I wasn't doing it. I can't even think that fast. The words were pouring out and God's love was pouring over me.

I went to a meeting of the Full Gospel Businessmen's Fellowship at the Lake of the Ozarks. I was pretty well known across the State of Missouri in Baptist circles, but I figured no Baptist that I knew would be there. I got in there and I couldn't believe what I was seeing! HERE WERE GROWN MEN HUGGING ONE ANOTHER! I couldn't believe this. There was love flowing all over! I sat down and relaxed . . . but not for long. "Why Dr. Horner." I didn't get by unrecognized. The President of the Springfield, Missouri chapter got up and said, "I've got some exciting news to tell you." He said, "There is a young professor, a Bible professor, who has been baptized in the Holy Spirit. This man has written a book against speaking in tongues. He got up in one of his classes the other day and ripped the book to shreds and said, 'This book will never go to press.' "

I said, "Mmm. I wonder who that is."

He said, "The man has spoken all over Missouri . . . churches have used him, as he has gone around to speak against the business of tongues and the baptism in the Holy Spirit." I had been around in churches speaking on the fullness of the Holy Spirit and so on, and I was still wondering who he was talking about. He continued, "He teaches at Southwest Baptist College."

I began to sink down into my chair a little bit.

"His name is Dr. Jerry Horner," he said.

I knew what was coming next. I just knew he was going to say, "He's here tonight." And I knew that I wasn't even supposed to be there! The fellows with me were just dying laughing. Praise God, it turned out that the brother had no idea I was there. He had never met me before, and he got his testimony twisted just a little bit.

One day while I was driving to Springfield, I felt a strong compulsion to stop at a particular Christian book store. I thought "I don't have time to stop here. I've got an appointment." But the compulsion was so strong, I stopped and browsed around and overheard two ladies speaking. One lady said to the other, "I don't remember the exact title of this book, but it has the word 'Praise' in it." That interested me, and I looked down right where I was standing; and here was the book with the title PRAISE THE LORD, ANYWAY.

I said, "Is this the book you're looking for?"

She said, "Oh yes, do you know anything about the lady who wrote this book?"

"No."

She told me something about her, so I picked up a couple of the books, PRAISE THE LORD, ANYWAY and HOT LINE TO HEAVEN. After I read those books I went back and got the rest of the books written by Charles and Frances Hunter. Shortly thereafter I read in the paper that Charles and Frances were going to be in Springfield at the Full Gospel meeting. I figured I could get a wig and dark glasses and go over there.

Right before I went to that meeting, I read about a

newspaper reporter in Minneapolis who was not a Christian who went out to cover a Lutheran charismatic convention. He said he saw somebody pray for a person with one leg shorter than the other and RIGHT BEFORE HIS EYES THE LEG GREW! This man was not even a Christian. He was a newspaper reporter, and he wasn't trying to prove anything. He was just stating facts!

I went to the meeting that night. My wife received the baptism in the Holy Spirit. Afterward I went up to Charles Hunter and said, "Brother Hunter, I wish you would pray for my back. I've got terrible back problems. Sometimes I can't even straighten up. My neck is so stiff. My shoulders are so stiff."

He looked at me, "Did it ever occur to you that your trouble might be that you've got one leg shorter than the other?"

I said, "Oh no."

He said, "Well, let's check it out."

I sat down in a straight chair, took my shoes off, and stuck my legs out. Sure enough, my right leg was about 3/4 inch shorter than the left one. Before I knew what he was doing, he was asking the Lord to lengthen the leg and, boom, out it came!

The next day I told my best friend what had happened. You know how that went over? He's a Baptist preacher. I though he'd be excited about this! I thought he would rejoice!

He said, "I think you ought to see a psychiatrist."

I said, "I already have. His name is Jesus."

Last October, I was walking across the campus on the way to the Greek class, and the Lord stopped me dead in my tracks. He said, "You're going to Oral Roberts University to teach." I had never even thought about the place. I had never been there. I knew very little about it except its reputation for being an excellent institution in every way. But the Lord said, "You're going to Oral Roberts University to teach." I put the thought aside. I didn't mention it to anybody. This was before some turmoil at the college where I was teaching took place.

The Lord was getting me ready to move. I was told that I would be restricted in my movements, that I couldn't attend meetings of the Full Gospel Business Men's Fellowship, that I couldn't mention the baptism. I told the Lord that night, "Lord, if you're getting me ready to leave, I not only am ready to leave, I want to leave. I pray that you'll open a place for me at Oral Roberts University."

The very next day I got a telephone call from Oral Roberts University. I had not applied there. The Holy Spirit had already spoken because the recommendation came from Charles and Frances Hunter.

Many Christians are suffering from various forms of spiritual weakness, simply because they've never grasped what the Holy Spirit can be in their lives. We're always going to stand powerless and abashed in the presence of our difficulties and our enemies until we experience the Holy Spirit as a mighty kind of flood power of love within our lives. Before Jesus left this world, in fact on the night of his betrayal, he said, "I will ask the Father, and he will give you another Comforter." When Jesus received the promise of the Spirit from the Father, he received him for you and me. At Pentecost, Peter explained that what happened there was meant not only for the apostles, but for those people present, "for as many as were afar off, even as many as the Lord would call." Jesus Christ gave the Holy Spirit to his church to be its permanent possession during this present age, and the Lord Jesus Christ is waiting to give each individual member of that church his or her share in Pentecost on the one condition, of applying for it by faith. There are thousands of Christians who are living on this side of Pentecost, as if that great event had never occurred. They're living on the same plane as those early disciples before they were filled with the Holy Spirit. Historically and chronologically, they are living on this side; but experientially they are living on the other side of Pentecost.

The river of God just flows on and on in its glorious fullness; but how tragic it is that many professing Christians have withdrawn from the banks of that river and are content to live on the edge of an arid desert. How foolish it is to forsake the fountains of living water to go to cisterns that can hold none. Wouldn't it be foolish for a man to refuse the uses of electricity and be content to go on in the same old way of past centuries; but those who are content to live their life without the power which is right there within reach are making the same mistake. People say they want to live like Christ. They want to follow in his steps. Yet, they refuse to make use of the power which he himself has supplied. The Pentecostal fullness, the enduement of power, the baptism of fire are all within our reach; and I pray that we'll be inspired with a holy ambition to get all that our Lord is willing to bestow.

Luke chapter 4 tells us about the relationship of the Holy Spirit to the Lord Jesus Christ. He went to the Jordan and was baptized, and there he was filled with the Holy Spirit. He went in the fullness of the Holy Spirit into the desert to be tempted, and he returned to Galilee in the power of the Holy Spirit. He stood up in the synagogue in Nazareth and declared that the Spirit of God was upon him, and we're told in Acts 10:38 that the wondrous works and words of Jesus are directly traced to the marvelous operation of the Holy Spirit upon his human life. Our Savior would not begin to help a dying, broken-hearted world until he was sure he had the power of the Spirit of God.

It is absurd for us to send our young men to college and to seminary to equip them with an intellectual and philosophical and grammatical learning and then to send them out to preach and to teach without insisting that if

Jesus himself waited to be anointed before he went to preach, NO YOUNG MAN OUGHT TO PREACH UNTIL HE HAS BEEN ANOINTED OF THE HOLY SPIRIT. Jesus promised that same power to his followers, ALL OF THEM. Just as you took forgiveness from the hand of the dying Savior, you can take your share of the Pentecostal gift from the hand of the living Savior. Don't think that the blessed gift of the Holy Spirit is reserved for some spiritual super stars or for some special work. The fullness of the Spirit of God is meant for EVERY BELIEVER to make them the disciples they ought to be. The failure of so many Christians is that they are trying to attain the ideal that God has set up for us without the power which alone makes the ideal possible.

The Holy Spirit has always been in this world. The same Holy Spirit who was at Pentecost was there at creation. It was that Spirit which brooded over the chaos. It was that Spirit who spoke through prophets and empowered saints of the Old Testament times. The day of Pentecost did not introduce a new Holy Spirit into the world. It began an era in which EVERY BELIEVER might possess him in the same measure as did those spiritual aristocrats who did live in the power of the Spirit of God before that day. What had been the prerogative of only a few, ones like Moses and Elijah and Isaiah and Daniel and so on, became the common property of every Christian. The ministry of the Holy Spirit is not the exclusive of any age. The gifts of the Holy Spirit are not limited to any confined epic in the history of the church. The Holy Spirit pours out his flood-tide of light and power around us today, and the Holy Spirit will enrich and fertilize the soil of any life which is willing to receive. How tragic it is that many people think that God is like some bankrupt builder, that he began building his church, that he built the portico of the church out of beautiful marble, but that he ran out and finished it with common clay brick. How tragic!

"Be filled with the Holy Spirit." That's a command. God's commandments are enablings! GOD IS PREPARED TO MAKE US WHAT HE TELLS US TO BECOME. Rejoice, because the fullness of the Holy Spirit is for you! YOU CAN NEVER EXPECT TO HAVE THE BAPTISM OF THE HOLY SPIRIT IF YOU ARE CONTENT TO LIVE WITHOUT IT. The Lord Jesus would not entrust this priceless gift to those who are indifferent to its possession. The promises of the scripture ought to incite us to the uttermost so that we will desire the Holy Spirit; that rivers of living water should flow from within; that we should be taught all things and be led into the whole circle of truth; that we should know Jesus Christ and be transformed into his image; that we should have assurance and power. All of this ought to be so fascinating that it seems impossible not to burn with the holy desire to be filled with the Holy Spirit. Our one passion must be the glory of the Lord Jesus Christ, and our only one purpose must be to magnify him, whether by life or by death.

I want to give you five tests, briefly, by which you may KNOW that you have received this infilling. You'll understand all of this presupposes the fact that you are a Christian. A person cannot have the ABUNDANT life without first experiencing life itself, and you cannot walk in newness of life until first you have been resurrected to new life.

Here are the tests: First, is the Lord Jesus Christ a living reality in your life? Jesus said in John 16 that the Holy Spirit would glorify him. How tragic that many Christians have a past-tense Savior.

When I was a boy I used to hear these testimony meetings, and I noticed several things. For one thing, the same people always talked. For another thing they always said the same thing. For another thing, it was always in the past tense, how God saved them. This is tremendous that we look back on our experience with the Lord, but what about today?

There are many people who have a future tense Savior. They anticipate the Lord's return. We ought to do this! But what about the present tense Savior? Jesus is in the NOW. He is a present, living reality and there are so many Christians who have no perception of Christ as a living presence with them day by day and moment by moment. When the Spirit of God fills the heart, Jesus is vividly real and evidently near. The whole aim of the Holy Spirit is to shed light upon Jesus Christ. The Spirit does not glorify himself, he does not reveal himself, but Jesus. So the person who is most filled with the Spirit of God talks most about Jesus as a living personality in his presence.

I have a Baptist pastor friend who was fired not too long ago because he was baptized in the Holy Spirit. Do you know what one of the complaints against him was? Can you believe this from a Baptist deacon? He said, "All he talks about is Jesus."

I know of another Baptist pastor who was fired. The church gave him an opportunity to give his side of the story. He got up and for a solid hour he quoted scripture. At the conclusion the chairman of deacons got up and said, "Well, Brother So-and-so, it may be scriptural; but it's not Baptistic."

What is Jesus Christ to you? Do you awake in the morning beneath his light touch? Do you spend the hours of the day with him, conscious of his presence? Are you constantly seeking and receiving from him power and grace and direction? Do you have a total awareness of his presence? If Christ is just a dim vision in your life way back or way off, then you have not realized the Pentecostal gift!

A second test is this: Do you have assurance that you ARE a child of God? Paul said the Holy Spirit seals us. The Holy Spirit is our earnest, our pledge, our guarantee of our redemption. His sacred office is to witness with our spirit that we ARE the children of God. He's the Spirit of adoption whereby we cry "Abba, Father." The Holy Spirit brings us an assurance of salvation that is quite independent of our emotions and our feelings. Many people have a roller coaster religion. They are up, and they are down. If I had to depend upon my feelings for my security in God I'd have been swept away long ago, but there is a deeper consciousness in the fullness of the Holy Spirit which your feelings do not affect.

A third test is: Do you have victory over known sin? What did Paul say? Walk in the Spirit, and you will not fulfill the lusts of the flesh. That negative in the Greek text is the strongest way of negating. It's a double negative. You'll not ever fulfill the lusts of the flesh. You'll not carry it out. I don't ask if you're sinless. I know the answer to that already, but are you kept from known sin up to the light God has given you? IF YOU ARE CONSTANTLY BEING OVERCOME, YOU'RE NOT FILLED WITH THE HOLY SPIRIT. The Holy Spirit is like an antiseptic to impure thoughts and unclean desires and things that are selfish and worldly and abominable. When the Holy Spirit fills the heart with his glorious fullness, the suggestions of temptation are instantly quenched like sparks in water. The Holy Spirit is the antidote to the dominion of the flesh. Sin can no more stand against the presence of the Holy Spirit than darkness can resist the all pervasive beams of the bright morning sun.

The Christian life is not legalistic. It doesn't consist in avoiding this and that and performing this rule or regulation, but the Christian life consists of being so saturated with something better that you have no desire for those simple, sinful things.

If you're full of the Spirit of God you're delivered from the power of sin. You'll be kept full of Jesus Christ and holy desires, and the epidemic of sin will have no fascination over you. There are many Christians who say they just can't give up "that" habit, they can't rid themselves of "that" thing which grips them. Would God give us an ideal and then leave us to ourselves to wallow in the swamp of our own helplessness and impunity? Jesus Christ is not a theory to be studied; he's a living power in one's life.

The fourth test is: Do you have power to witness? Didn't Jesus tell his disciples that when this power came upon them they would bear witness to him? Can you speak to others for the Lord Jesus Christ? Do you have a burning thirst for the salvation of others? Have you ever agonized over the alienation of anyone from God? Is it natural for you to speak for Jesus? Or is it an effort for you to witness for him? It isn't difficult for a bird to sing. It isn't difficult for a child to laugh. It shouldn't be difficult for you to speak for Jesus Christ. You cannot expect fruit to fall into your basket and fish to break your net until you obtain the power that Jesus promised. If you are living in Christ and Christ lives in you, living waters ought to spring up and overflow and splash on others.

The fifth test is: Do you have the Spirit of holy love? I love the last few verses of Acts 2, because they give us a tremendous description of the life of the early church. Do you remember how they were going around sharing things, how they were filled with love and joy? Is there bitterness, jealousy, strife and selfishness instead of kindness and mutual helpfulness and unity and humility? If only we were filled with the Holy Spirit, then there would be joy, a power, a consciousness of the Lord Jesus, and a habitual rest in the will of God. I ask you to refuse to be satisfied with anything less than the full indwelling of God's Holy Spirit. The great tragedy is that so many Christians are spiritual window shoppers. They walk along the spiritual avenue, and look at all the priceless treasures of God displayed there. Did you know there is not a price tag on any of them? They all say, "my free gift." They look at that and say, "That's terrific! That's great!" But they never have faith to believe the promise of God to reach out and take the priceless gifts of God!

Let me give you five steps to help you in your faith.
1. Say THERE IS SUCH A BLESSING AS THE BAPTISM OF THE HOLY SPIRIT. I've tried to show you that that blessing is there. There IS such a thing as the baptism in the Holy Spirit.
2. IT IS FOR ME. Believe that it is for you. If words mean anything at all, then the Pentecostal experience is for us today. There is as much Holy Spirit power today as there ever was, and God does not reserve that power for a few of his favorites and then leave the rest to take their chance.
3. I HAVE NOT GOT IT. Realize that you don't have it. Do you recognize that although you may exhibit and display the power of intellect and energy and enthusiastic zeal, there is a lack in your life?
4. I'M WILLING TO SECURE IT AT ALL COSTS, and I am prepared to surrender whatever hinders me from receiving all that God has for me.
5. I HUMBLY AND THANKFULLY OPEN MY HEART TO RECEIVE ALL that I believe my Savior is waiting to give.

Do you know what somebody said to me the other day? "Boy, you've really gone off the deep end." I said, "Praise the Lord, you can't learn to swim until you get in water over your head." I have seen terrific miracles of God since I received the baptism. One morning I called my mother who is over the age of seventy. She is in poor health; we've been praying for her. We have full confidence that the Lord is going to give her an overhaul; but last week when I called her, I knew something was wrong because my father answered the phone. I learned that my mother had had a hemorrhage behind her left eye. She couldn't do anything. She couldn't get up suddenly, because the rush of blood might even be fatal. She couldn't do her housework. She couldn't get out of the house. She couldn't do anything.

A few days ago I felt impressed to call Mother and just pray for over the telephone. We'd been lifting her up in prayer. I talked to her and over the phone I prayed the Lord's healing upon her. I hadn't heard from her since those several days ago until I called her this morning. She said, "Well, I haven't called you back because I didn't know whether you'd be home. As soon as I hung up the phone the other day and turned around something came over me." She said, "The power of God came over me. The pain is gone. The spot is disappearing. I can do my housework. I went to church." People were surprised. She couldn't even get out of the house, under doctor's orders. She went to church just beaming. The people said, "What happened to you?" She said, "I told them."

My entire spiritual life has been revolutionized by the baptism of the Holy Spirit and my ministry has been drastically changed for the better. Jesus Christ became evidently near and vividly real to me. I had known Jesus as my Savior for most of my life, but he was always so in the background. More and more Jesus became a living reality; and I enjoyed a moment by moment relationship with him as I practiced the Presence of God.

The function of the Holy Spirit is to bear witness to Christ, to glorify him. He certainly did that in my life! I began to experience the power of God. I had read about signs and wonders following the teaching of the word but had never seen any of that in my ministry. But now, more and more manifestations of the power of God were becoming manifest in my own ministry. I began to see miracles take place in my own life and in the lives of members of my family and in the lives of people to whom I ministered.

The baptism in the Holy Spirit brought new areas of spiritual understanding in my life. The Bible is no longer merely a textbook, but it has become a living word to me! I have a greater appreciation for the grace of God in saving me. I have a greater appreciation for the work of others. I now see people as individuals, objects of God's love, people for whom Christ gave the supreme sacrifice. I have a compassion and a love for them. My greatest desire is to know him better, to love him more, and to be transformed into his image in a greater degree. The baptism in the Holy Spirit for me was not the end of my Christian goal, but only the beginning, because the Spirit of God has opened my eyes to see how much more there is!

Ann

Has your Christian life not been very exciting? Have you wondered what in the world is wrong? Have you been bored? Have you looked around and said, "Lord, is this all there is to Christianity?" About four years ago this is just where I was in my walk with the Lord. For years I had cried out and cried out to the Lord, "Lord, what is wrong? Is this all there is to Christianity?" I was very busy in my Christian walk. I was Sunday School teacher, busy in the W.M.U. at the Baptist Church, busy at Training Union, constantly busy doing God's work. Still there was a hunger in my life, a hunger I didn't quite understand. I BLAMED MY PASTOR FOR NOT HAVING THE SPIRITUAL GROWTH THAT I LACKED IN MY LIFE. I thought he wasn't feeding me spiritually. I sat at church Sunday after Sunday, Sunday after Sunday, bored.

My husband (Jerry) taught at Southwest Baptist College for about eleven years. After he had been there seven years he had his Sabbatical, and we went to England. While we were there we met this beautiful English Christian couple, and their Christian life was very, very exciting. This even made me question more and more, "Why, Lord? Why? Why is their life exciting and ours is not?" We came back to the States, and I was worse off than ever. In the fall of 1970 they came to see us, and they thought, "Here we are in the Bible Belt, and we really are going to see Christianity at its very best." But when they got to our town, Ballwin, Missouri, they told us, "It is spiritually dead here! Doesn't Satan ever tempt you? Doesn't Satan ever cause you any problems?" I looked at Pauline, and I said, "Satan? What do you mean, 'Satan causes problems'?" She said, "If Satan is not causing you any problems, you had better check your spiritual walk." This question stayed in my mind more and more.

During this time also my husband was going through a very trying struggle with the Lord. I didn't know what was wrong, because he completely ignored me and the children. It was a hard time, and I felt like sometimes I'd just like to take my life, because I didn't think life was worth living.

Then, in the fall of 1972, Jerry received the baptism. He didn't tell me about it, but the students knew by the way he talked there was something very different in his teaching. He had shared with his friend, and by way of the grapevine it got back to me that he had tongues. This upset me greatly because he didn't share it with me first. I got very, very upset.

I had a friend who I heard "spoke in tongues." I went up to her and said, "What is this all about? I don't understand it." She gave me a whole stack of books to read. I read all the books I could find and did exactly what they said to do to receive the baptism, but nothing happened! The Lord brought Frances Hunter's books into our lives at this time and I had read everyone of those. In December of 1972 we noticed in the Springfield, Missouri, paper that the Hunters were going to be at the Full Gospel meeting. We had some friends take care of our children, and Friday night, December 18, 1972, we went to hear Frances and Charles. I was very, very amazed at all the things they had to say and all the things that went on. After the meeting was over I told Jerry, "You go call our friends and tell them we're going to be late, because I want Frances to pray for me." I went up to Frances that night and said, "Frances, I want to accept the baptism with the Holy Spirit." She prayed for me at that time, I received the baptism of the Holy Spirit, and my prayer language just flowed out.

God really has a sense of humor, because the next night when we went to the Hunters' meeting, they had all of us measure our arms to see if we had a short one! I couldn't believe what I saw, because one of my arms was about four inches shorter than the other. I had never been aware of this, but after measuring and remeasuring, the arm was still four inches shorter. They were praying from the platform, and right in front of Jerry's and my eyes, MY ARM GREW OUT to be exactly the same length as the other one and is exactly the same today!

Since that night, my life has become an adventure with Jesus Christ! From that day forth I no longer had to say my Christian life was boring. JESUS HAS BECOME REAL TO ME. His love and God's love have become personal and genuine to me!

I had a lot of hangups. I felt very insecure, unloved, unwanted; but Jesus has delivered me from this. Isn't it beautiful how Jesus will just show us a little bit at a time, the ugly things in our lives we need to turn over to him. He doesn't take us through it all at once and show us ALL the dirt, but he shows us a little at a time. I praise the Lord for this. I praise the Lord that he has been able to use the Jesus in me day by day to minister to others. He has led me into a ministry of deliverance and inner healing. I know in my own power that I could not do this, but through the power of Jesus Christ our Savior have I been able to minister to people.

I have found out in this new walk that all God wants of us is our availability. Be available in all things to him. A young boy was once asked, "What does 'Immanuel' mean?" He said, "It means 'interrupted.'" Do you realize that Jesus interrupted his time in heaven to be here with us? So we have to be willing to have our lives interrupted so that we can be used of Jesus to serve others.

The main thing in this Christian life that I want is to be able to minister to my family. The verse that comes to me is Psalm 101:2 in the Living Bible: "I will try to walk a blameless path, but how I need your help, especially in my own home, where I long to act as I should." And I do long to act as I should in my own home. Only the Holy Spirit ministering to me can make me act the way I should. My Christian life, as I said before, has been very, very exciting since this new walk with Jesus. The baptism of the Holy Spirit has added a new dimension to my life I had never known. I praise the Lord for my prayer language, because without it I would not know how to pray sometimes. All I have to do is pray in the Spirit, and the Holy Spirit tells me how to pray. It's not only the prayer language, it's not only tongues, but I rejoice that I have more and more of the love of Jesus, and I thank God for this!

BARBARA JEAN SONNTAG

"After having been at the Catholic services, this was really different. I WAS SCARED TO DEATH! I have been set free from so much of my past life and traditionalism."

"And we all hear these men telling in our own languages about the mighty miracles of God! " Acts 2:11 (TLB)

Barbara Jean, SCARED TO DEATH, as she puts it, now excitedly tells about the mighty miracles of God. She will tell you in English, but perhaps her spirit praises God in her Spirit language for his mighty miracles in her life and family.
Listen!

I have been a Catholic for thirty-eight years; was raised and educated in the Catholic faith. I was married at twenty-one, started my family and tried to grow into an adult. Leaving California, our family came to Colorado to start our new home and life — which I believe was the work of God. We moved against great odds, but our faith and obedience to God pulled us through and prepared us for the great victory in Jesus which our family is now enjoying.

It all started November 24, 1974, when a group of Christian people paid the way for our entire family to see the movie, "A Time to Run." Something wonderful happened there: I accepted Jesus as my personal Savior. A Pentecostal woman was the one God had chosen to witness to me. This was all new because we, as Catholics, were not accustomed to doing things like this in our church.

The woman invited me to attend interdenominational Bible services, but I always found some excuse not to go. One day she was so persistent I asked her to come to my home after the service, and I would talk with her. Wow! What a day! It was January 17, 1975, and not one but TWO Pentecostals came to my home and gave me the works! After they left, I felt moved to read the Bible they gave me and inside was neatly tucked away a little booklet saying something about receiving the Holy Spirit. I wasn't too sure what this was all about, but I read it anyway. WHAT DID I HAVE TO LOSE?

I read the booklet and guess what? The Holy Spirit visited me, I committed my life to Jesus Christ and from that moment my whole life began to change. My family wasn't too excited; they thought this was something I had decided to do and then drop, like everything else in my life. Well, I sure didn't drop anything! It just got better and better.

I had experienced back pain for the last twelve years,

and no doctors really knew what was wrong. I had been in and out of hospitals and had been given all kinds of tests. Last year I went to work in a nursing home. While employed there I injured my back severely and was hospitalized. The doctors couldn't help, but I found a wonderful man who gave me therapy. I recovered enough to go back to work. Well, I did return and injured my back once again. I was forced to quit my job and seek other employment. I suffered pain all the time. I had decided if the Lord wanted my back healed, he would do it in his own time, and I tried to accept my situation.

Last February I learned that the Hunters, Charles and Frances, would be coming to Grand Junction, Colorado, to evangelize. There were reports that wherever they went many healings occurred. I heard they would be here May 10, which was my sister's birthday. I JUST HAD TO FIND A WAY TO GET THERE! I knew the Lord was going to do something great that night, and I was sure it would be my back! Oh, the joy of never having to suffer awful back pain again!

In the next few weeks, I was invited to go to a Pentecostal revival where my boss attended church. I went with some fellow workers, and after having been at the Catholic services, this was really different. I WAS SCARED TO DEATH! I shook the whole two hours, but I did what everyone else did. I kept going back but making sure I also attended our church so my family wouldn't get angry. It was really a sacrifice sometimes, but I am glad I went. This was my introduction into the Spirit-filled life. I learned new songs, how to worship, and a feeling of really belonging. For the first time in my life my spirit was free. It was nice to worship and praise the Lord out loud. What a beautiful experience. I was able to take my oldest boy and girl a couple of times to the revival, but my husband soon put his foot down and said that all of this was some kind of "HOLY ROLLER THING." Well, I didn't argue, and I'm glad

I didn't, because my husband let me go to the rally on May 10. You sure guessed right — it was a night I will NEVER forget!

This whole service was held at the First Assembly of God Church, 4th and Grand, Grand Junction, Colorado, just two blocks from our own church. I walked in with a good friend of mine, and we sat near the front so we wouldn't miss anything. Oh! there was a lot of singing, praising, and warm fellowship. There came a point in the service where the Lord actually started to do great healings. I sat there waiting, not too patiently. Then it happened! A great heat went through my body and Frances said someone had just had their back healed. My friend yelled, "That's you, that's you!" and I said, "It couldn't be!" I jumped around, wiggled, and twisted. I felt no pain but a warm heat in my back. IT WASN'T EMOTION EITHER, IT WAS REAL!!

I ran up on the stage and waited my turn at the platform to testify to the truth of the injury and healing.

All of a sudden something very strange happened. I was seeing something as a Catholic I hadn't seen before; people falling down on the ground. I didn't know what was going on so I asked what it was. I was told that these people were "falling under the power of God" or being "slain in the Spirit." What funny words these were; I had never heard or seen this before. NOW, I WAS REALLY SCARED TO DEATH! Would they do this to me? If they did it wouldn't work because anyone who knows me knows I have a terrible fear of falling and I WAS SURE THERE WAS SOME HOCUS POCUS INVOLVED.

These people sure must be emotional because of their healings, I thought. I'll keep my cool and show them! I sat down and some funny sounds were coming out of my mouth. Frances ran over, because it was my turn next at the platform and said to Charles he ought to forget me, that I was receiving the baptism of the Holy Spirit. I got up, went to the platform, gave my testimony and before you could say ' boo! '' these people were standing in front of me, speaking in unknown languages and THERE I WAS ON THE FLOOR. Wow! This was real and I started to shake all over. Somehow, later I managed to get back to my seat. I was a mess but I loved every moment!

It came time for the altar call, and my friend wanted to go so I went with him for moral support. That's a laugh, because we both marched out to the prayer room, and together we received the full baptism of the Spirit. What a night! I shall never forget the joy in my soul! Could a human dare to be this happy?

Well that was only the beginning. The next night, same time and place, Betty Baxter, a great evangelist for the Lord, was there. The Lord found a way for my thirteen-year-old daughter and I to go. We had just come home from an outing in the mountains and some dunebug riding. (Yes, I went dunebug riding for two hours over real bumpy roads and my back never hurt at all.) What a victory for Jesus, because people with injured backs just don't do that. I did, because my back was healed. Hallelujah! Anyhow, my daughter and I attended the service and when the altar call was given she went forward, accepted Jesus as her personal Savior and Lord, then marched to the prayer room, received the baptism of the Spirit and spoke in tongues. Wow! that's not all, the next night my husband permitted all the children to go and two more, the twelve and ten-year-old boys went forward and accepted Jesus. The family countdown was starting fast. Just two more, my husband and fourteen-year-old boy, who was a very lost and rebellious teenager. My five-year-old girl didn't count, she was still innocent.

I started attending every service I could get to because I was hungry for the WORD, and really fired up for the Lord. We all prayed at the church for my family and one day my husband said he would attend church the next

Sunday. We went and yes, he knelt down, repented and accepted Jesus!

The church people then made arrangements for all my children to go to summer camp. My thirteen and fourteen-year-olds went first. The boy accepted Jesus, received the baptism of the Spirit and was told by Jesus (while slain in the Spirit) that he would be an evangelist. Wow! from May 10 to June 15!! THE LORD SURE WAS WORKING OVERTIME IN OUR LITTLE CATHOLIC HOME. We were becoming Spirit-filled Pentecostals awfully fast, and all of us like it. My other two boys went to camp next, and they too came home Spirit-filled. This is all really wonderful. God is so good!

On June 20, I had an appointment for my glaucoma check by the eye doctor. Glaucoma was discovered about eighteen months before. After an examination, the doctor informed me that the condition I'd once had was gone! Wow! Isn't God good? He took care of everything for me. I must be checked again in six months, but I don't care because I know what will happen. My eyes will be perfect just the way Jesus fixed them. He is such a fine physician. He can work on me anytime!

Well, there you are, the exciting testimony of God's power in my family. My husband WILL become Spirit-filled! He is a fine Christian husband and father. Our family is so glad to be a part of the family of God and so thankful he has forgiven us. He has blessed us beyond our imagination. For the first time in my life I also learned to tithe. Oh! It is so much fun. Since then the blessings the Lord has sent down, both spiritual and material, are greater than words can say. Someone once told me to try to outgive God. I can't, he HAS more than I can give.

One thing I feel I really must include in this testimony is the great peace and freedom I feel since accepting Jesus as my personal Savior and Lord and being filled with the Holy Spirit. I have been set free from so much of my past life and so much traditionalism. Jesus has sent me the Comforter and with his help my body is infused with the Spirit. I now can walk freely and know Jesus lives in me. It's great being a Christian and to truly try to live as Christ. I praise God for loving me and my family so much!

I am excited about the future God has in store for us and the fire of living we now enjoy. I hope the fire of our family will touch someone else and let them know that the beautiful God we know also knows them!

Author's Note: Barbara Jean's husband received the baptism of the Holy Spirit, spoke in tongues and is filled to overflowing as his whole family is complete in Jesus!

MILTON L. HAMON

"I FELT GOD HAD LET US DOWN!..."
"No longer were we trying to disprove anything, but seeking only the truth. We wanted all of what God had for his children, NO MATTER WHAT PRICE WE HAD TO PAY. To me what really counts is the every day, abiding, comforting presence of the Holy Spirit; knowing that God's Holy Spirit now dwells within me, teaching and correcting, eliminating and comforting, and maturing me as a person."

Graduate of Gulf Coast Bible College, Houston, Texas. Attended Anderson College, Anderson, Indiana and University of Houston, Houston, Texas. Ordained to the ministry in the Church of God of Anderson, Indiana.

Charles was well acquainted with the minister parents of Milton and his two brothers, Wayne and Ray, when he was a teenage boy in West Texas. Their lives have been interwoven in church affiliation since then.

I (Charles) have seen a persistent desire in the hearts of these three brothers all these years to serve God. But

like me, there was a long, dry struggle to survive the effort to be a Christian . . . .
 U N T I L !

The baptism in the Holy Spirit brought a whole new way of life to me. It was the opening of a new door. When I look back I realize that God had been dealing with our family for a number of years. He had been directing our lives so that we could come to believe in the reality of such a relationship.

As a very young person I had felt God's hand on my life. At the age of twenty I felt a call into the Christian ministry and entered Bible school and college where I prepared myself that I might serve the Lord. I was ordained to the ministry in 1952 in the Church of God of Anderson, Indiana. I pastored in Louisiana, Alabama, and Texas for a number of years. Because of the name, our denomination was always confused with other churches which were Pentecostal. As a pastor I was always on the defensive and quick to explain we were not "THAT KIND OF A CHURCH." My mind was completely closed to the reality of a devotional language in connection with the baptism with the Holy Spirit. God had to deal with me for some time in order to open my mind to his word.

In 1967 my wife, our three sons, and our daughter were in Alabama where I was pastoring a church. We had been provided with an excellent parsonage, and I received a good salary. I had been elected three years before to the city council. No other preacher had ever been elected to such public office before in that part of the state, although a number had tried. But THERE WAS STILL SOMETHING MISSING IN OUR LIVES. So we resigned our church, and I resigned the seat on the city council. We moved back to Houston, Texas, where I entered the construction business. I continued to preach and to teach as opportunity presented itself, but within a year a simple test that was a surgical procedure was to explode into a most dreadful word to my wife, Patsy. The word was "cancer." IT COULDN'T HAPPEN TO US! We'd prayed. Our friends had prayed. After surgery and a long recovery, with still another surgery about eighteen months later, we were discouraged!

During this time our older boys lost interest in the church, and I FELT GOD HAD LET US DOWN. A little later when our oldest son became involved in some serious problems, we felt we were on the very bottom. In the midst of all this, we were called to pastor a small congregation in Conroe, Texas, and we felt happy to be back in God's service. I drove up on the weekend to preach, visit, and teach, then returned Sunday night after church. We continued to support ourselves as superintendent on a construction job there in the area. Our oldest sons had gone their own way, and we began to put everything we had into trying to build a church. We soon realized that we weren't getting much accomplished. We realized a need of more REAL power in our lives. We were becoming very dissatisfied with our own spiritual depth.

Early in 1973, as a routine matter, I received a letter to all pastors of our denomination. To me this letter said that Charles and Frances Hunter were no longer to be recognized by our movement because they had begun to teach the receiving of the baptism of the Holy Spirit with the evidence of tongues. Patsy had read all of their books. Because of the letter from the church, out of curiosity she looked until she found the latest book they had written entitled THE TWO SIDES OF A COIN. She had hoped to learn more of their experience from reading this book. It wasn't very long until she presented me with the book. I said, "I know Charles and Frances Hunter, so I'll read this one."

This book really spoke to both of us. It answered a lot of questions that had been unanswered by my studies of systematic theology in college and by our doctrinal practice as ministers. I found several things in this book:

    1. That Paul wrote to the Corinthian Church for the purpose of giving them proper instructions in the

use of tongues, not to deny their reality and their existence.
2. That there are different kinds of tongues. There is a devotional tongue that only God understands, and there are tongues that need to be interpreted.

I really wanted the real thing, and this book opened our minds to the possibility of there being more to the baptism in the Holy Spirit than we had believed.

My faith was beginning to develop. One thing it did for us was that it caused us both to be determined to go to the Bible and study the word of God in order for us to really see what it said. But this time WE WERE GOING TO STUDY WITH AN OPEN MIND, so that we might in an objective way really search the scriptures to see what the truth of God's word was. No longer were we trying to disprove anything, but seeking only the truth. We studied for a number of weeks. Patsy fasted most of the time and I fasted some and we came to believe that God's word really taught the baptism with the Holy Spirit was accompanied by a praise language.

We never had been to a Pentecostal Church or a full gospel church of any kind. We'd never heard anyone speak in any kind of tongue, and we really didn't know what it was all about. I knew, too, that I wouldn't be able to continue to be a minister in our movement if I ever let anyone know that I had such an experience as this; but we wanted all of what God had for his children, NO MATTER WHAT PRICE WE HAD TO PAY. We began to pray for the baptism of the Holy Spirit with tongues.

The first week of June, 1973, I was in my daughter's bedroom, because she was out of the house at the time, and Patsy was in our bedroom next door praying. I prayed in faith to God, and I asked that he would fill me completely. This time I really believed that he would. I said, "Amen," and just waited silently and openly for what would happen next. Nothing happened except that I felt real good. I said, "Well, Lord, I know you heard my prayers, and I believe that you're going to answer me in whatever way and in whatever time you see fit about this."

The next day as I was going about my job, I heard singing from time to time and I really couldn't understand any of the words. When I'd stop and listen it kept on. This increased until almost any time I'd stop and be quiet and begin to listen I would hear this music coming from inside me. It was beautiful! It was like stereo music in 3-D! I seemed to be hearing a multitude of heavenly voices! It was God's angelic choir singing with ten thousand tongues, and I couldn't understand a one!

Later at a prayer meeting while others were praying in English, I just kind of joined silently in worshipping God with this angelic choir. This continued for several weeks, and Patsy wasn't getting very much results as far as her being able to really receive the baptism at this time. We really didn't know what to expect, anyway. We didn't know that we had to begin to speak by faith as the Holy Spirit gave the utterance.

One of our sons, who was living in California at the time, became hospitalized. We were worried, because we couldn't find out what had happened to him. His friends who called us the first time never called back. Patsy was real sick and worried, and so was I. She was lying down in bed with a severe headache. That night I knelt down by the bed, and laid my hands on her head and began to pray. I didn't pray in English! Words came out that I couldn't understand! ALL THE BARRIERS THAT I HAD BUILT UP AFTER ALL THESE YEARS WERE SWEPT AWAY BY THE LANGUAGE OF GOD'S SPIRIT. I really didn't know what I was praying, but I knew I was praying for Patsy's relief, and I was praying for our son's salvation and healing. When I stopped praying, Patsy looked at me in a strange way, and in a few minutes she got up and we walked out in the back yard together. Her head had quit hurting almost instantly.

I had received also at this time what must have been a word of knowledge, because I told her that I felt God was working through this to bring our son back home to see us, and that God was working to bring him to himself as Savior.

The next day Patsy felt that she would like to call and ask for prayer from Charles and Frances Hunter. She didn't know the number or how to call, but she looked up their number in an old telephone directory that we had and called them. Her mother was also facing surgery at this time, and the doctor had told her to prepare for the worst. We wanted to request prayer for her as well. I had already called a minister in our church yearbook that I didn't even know, and asked him to visit the hospital and see if he could visit our son and let us know about his condition.

When Patsy called the Hunters' number, Joan "by chance" was there and answered the phone. She is the daughter of Frances and Charles and was about the same age as our son. I believe she was just the one who needed to pray for our son at this time. She listened to Patsy's story about him, and told us that Charles and Frances were out of town. She prayed for both his healing and his salvation. When Patsy hung up the phone, she said, "I just believe that the Lord really heard this prayer and that God is really going to answer." He did, because THAT SAME NIGHT we got a call from California from the minister who had visited our son. He told us that he had prayed with him and that he was doing good. He had accepted Christ as his Savior and said he wanted to come home as soon as he could be released from the hospital.

Two of my brothers were being led by the Lord during this time also. My oldest brother Wayne had received the baptism of the Holy Spirit months before, but I had not talked with him prior to my receiving. I was working for another one of my brothers, Ray, who was Spirit-filled about the same time I was, but we didn't realize this until later when we shared our experience that the Lord was working in both of our lives at this same period of time.

Ray was interested in learning more about his recent baptism of the Spirit. He had learned through Wayne of the Hunter home prayer meetings. We all planned to attend the next month's meeting, but on this Thursday I had to travel out of town and did not return until too late to drive back to Houston from Conroe. Ray and Wayne had attended and they filled me in on all that had happened at the meeting.

During this talk I told them of Patsy's desire to be baptized in the Holy Spirit but that she had not as yet received. Ray and Wayne decided to pay her a visit the next day, so without telling me they called Patsy who told them to come over. When I drove in the drive that afternoon Patsy met me at the door. One look at her told me she had received the baptism. THERE WAS A GLOW ALL OVER HER. She told me how it happened!

Wayne and Ray arrived at about the time school was letting out and our 12-year-old daughter Connie was getting in. They told Patsy they had come to pray with her to receive the baptism. They went into the living room and began to talk. During the conversation our daughter arrived home from school and started to go into the living room. By this time my brothers had laid hands on Patsy and were praying for her to receive. Connie waited in the hall just outside the door but was looking in the room. Patsy immediately received her prayer language and the three began to pray in other tongues.

Connie was still in the hall observing this. She had read many of our charismatic books and had studied her Bible, so she just began to pray in the Spirit out in the hall, too. Patsy, Ray and Wayne didn't know what was happening to her. I had received praying for myself, Patsy received by "laying on of hands" and our daughter spontaneously. All in different ways, but the same Spirit, just as it had been experienced in the book of Acts.

To us the baptism in the Holy Spirit meant the loss of our pastorate, because four months later when I gave my testimony on a Sunday night to our church, telling about our new relationship, some of the people couldn't accept what had happened or THE EMBARRASSMENT OF HAVING A PASTOR WHO SPOKE IN AN UNKNOWN TONGUE. I resigned that night because I know God's word is true. One of these days, according to his word, we'll have a church a hundred times larger. The word of God says if you've left homes or houses or friends or land for Jesus' sake in this life you'll have a hundred times more, and in the life to come, eternal life. That's going to be some kind of church, and I can't wait until the Lord works this out!

To me the baptism in the Holy Spirit was another doorway into maturity. I'm a better person than I was. I see the Bible more clearly than I ever did before.

The baptism of the Holy Spirit is not just an experience, it's a relationship — a vital relationship with God. SPEAKING IN TONGUES IS A REALITY FOR THIS DAY AND TIME. The operation of the Holy Spirit and the gifts of the Holy Spirit are thrilling for us to see working in the body of Christ in these last days. But, as exciting as all this is, to me it's the every day, abiding, comforting presence of the Holy Spirit that means the most to me; knowing that God's Holy Spirit now dwells within me, teaching and correcting, eliminating and comforting, and maturing me as a person. To me, this is what really counts. This is what it means, and this is why the baptism of the Holy Spirit is a whole new door of maturity for me. Praise God!

JACK AND JEAN WOOD

Jack: "IT CHANGED ME AND MY FAMILY FROM DEATH TO LIFE — NEW LIFE IN CHRIST JESUS — WITH POWER."

Jean: ". . . It wasn't long before I became overwhelmed with the fact that God really loved me and had given me his Holy Spirit . . . there's a boldness within me to share Jesus!"

Jack
B.Th., Gulf Coast Bible College, Houston, Texas
AA (Associate Arts) Contra Costa Junior College, Richmond, Calif.
Served as Specialist in U.S. Army. Soldier of the Year, Wolfhound Regiment, 25th Division in Osaka, Japan.
Worked in the personnel field for several years.
Director of the 700 Club in Houston

Jean
Registered Nurse — Honolulu, Hawaii with further studies in San Jacinto College, Pasadena, Texas

Director of Nurses, Eastway General Hospital, Houston, Texas

"So, my fellow believers, long to be prophets so that you can preach God's message plainly; and never say it is wrong to 'speak in tongues'; however, be sure that everything is done properly in a good and orderly way." I Cor. 14:39-40 (TLB)

We could actually see fear on the face of Jean as her twin sister Joan stepped out to receive "tongues." We weren't sure how Jack reacted. The tongue is a very good and important part of the body. It announces the taste of all good (or bad) food and drink entering the body. Just because it tells my brain something is bitter, I don't think of my tongue as an enemy to be feared. It can be an enemy of God. But it should be a friend of God. Teaching against "tongues" has scared so many of us that fear is the bitter reaction. Jean found a friendly tongue when she gave its control to the Holy Spirit — she found her spirit could speak to God when she prayed in tongues.

Jack was drawn by the power of spontaneous love of Spirit-filled people away from the pull of negative teaching.

Is it worth it, Jack and Jean? Let them tell you the good news and if you haven't received this beautiful gift, it's available, FREE!

JACK AND JEAN WOOD

Jean

I was raised in a Christian home and accepted Jesus in my pre-teen years. Our family went to church, and I was taught all the things that God expected from his children, but I always found that I could never quite meet all the standards. Jack and I were married and as we went to Bible College and into the ministry, I found that there was even greater pressure to put forth the Christian image of the perfect pastor's wife. I really wanted to live pleasing to the Lord, but I found I just didn't have the power to do it. As a result I felt like a failure, and Jack and I began having problems in our marriage. I even left several times for a couple of days. I became convinced that I was unacceptable to God and even sat around contemplating suicide. I REACHED OUT FOR HELP SEVERAL TIMES, BUT FRANKLY I DIDN'T FIND ANYONE WHO HAD AN ANSWER.

Meanwhile, Jack had left the ministry and shortly thereafter we left the Church of God. We started attending a Nazarene Church. We were hoping to find something. We knew deep down inside that something was missing, but we just didn't know what it was. During the time we were attending the Nazarene Church I accepted my present job as Supervisor of Nurses and had the opportunity to meet Frances when she was a patient in the hospital. I knew immediately that she had a real, living relationship with Jesus. That's what I wanted, too, and didn't have.

My sister and I attended a prayer meeting at her home. For the first time I heard about the baptism in the Holy Spirit. I was frightened, because I knew that Jack had preached against speaking in tongues. I didn't receive the baptism that night . . . I didn't even seek the baptism. In fact, if my sister hadn't been so insistent that we stay during the whole meeting, I PROBABLY WOULD HAVE RUN AWAY.

Charles and Frances mentioned a meeting at Evangelistic Temple. Jack and I visited the church. When we got there we saw in the people such a love, and there was such a move of the Spirit, we knew that this was what God wanted for us. After attending there for several weeks and being taught, we found ourselves in the chapel to accept the baptism in the Holy Spirit. At first I didn't really know what I had but it wasn't long before I became overwhelmed with the fact that God really loved me and had given me his Holy Spirit.

That was the real stabilizing point for me as I began to realize how much he loved me. Now I had the power to live the way I knew he wanted me to. There were still some ups and downs and with the maturity that we gained with the teaching at the Temple and with personal Bible reading and meditating, the ups and downs are getting further apart and not really so far up and down as they used to be.

Since I've received the baptism with the Holy Spirit, I've found that there's a boldness within me to share Jesus. I've been really pleased to see that a number of my coworkers have become saved and also filled with the Spirit. God has also touched our marriage relationship, and Jack and I are finding a oneness in the Spirit that we didn't have before. Our three children are filled with the Spirit, and are growing in the Lord also. In fact, our whole family is now surrounded with a love and unity instead of the bickering and fighting that we used to have.

As I look back over our lives, I can see that God was leading us to this experience of the fullness of the Spirit and a total devotion to him. I ONLY WISH WE HAD FOUND IT A WHOLE LOT SOONER.

Jack

Jean has laid it out pretty reasonably as far as our family is concerned. As far as my life personally is concerned, I think I was like Charles' description of his pre-Jesus life — spiritually (as well as carnally) a dried-up prune.

I was saved while in college where I was studying

Electronic Engineering. I went in the military service after that and married Jean while in the Hawaiian Islands.

It was in Hawaii that I heard of the baptism of the Holy Spirit. A young Christian met me in a park one time and we were just talking. He shared about the baptism with me but I kind of froze up. It wasn't for me, I thought. Had I accepted it then, it would have been so much sweeter for so much longer!

We knew by the time we were discharged from military service that the Lord wanted us to go into the ministry, so we attended and graduated from a Bible College. That made about eight years of college. We began pastoring in Port Arthur, Texas and loved the people there but we demanded justice when seemingly we were done injustice. We didn't know how to lay down our lives. When God showed us in Timothy that we were not to strive with his people, we left the pastorate and began in other lines of work, still working in a church, still leading people to Christ but doing it in the flesh, not in the Spirit, not as God moved . . . and still defeated.

When we were preaching in Port Arthur, we preached against the baptism in the Holy Spirit and speaking in tongues. We believed in the sanctification of the Holy Spirit, because that was Church of God doctrine, but we preached against tongues. We've always believed in miracles, signs and wonders, and the healings that God could bring because we felt this was scriptural.

It was when we began attending Evangelistic Temple that we first saw spontaneous love among people who had received the baptism. That was refreshing to us and we saw miracles happening which we hadn't seen before. I asked, "God, do you suppose I could have been wrong for so long?" I could feel by the witness of the Spirit that he was saying, "Yes, you know you have been." Praise God, we listened, heard and obeyed and received the baptism of the Holy Spirit. The baptism turned on a praise dimension inside us that opened a whole new spiritual world filled with the power Jesus promised and an abundant life of love and joy. As we praised him we felt his presence as never before.

The Holy Spirit-given prayer language gave us access to the Father and his presence and an anointing in a way we had never been familiar with before. It gave us a spiritual discernment of the scriptures. We began to see in the word great truths that we hadn't applied in our lives, and caused us to want to apply them. All our family relationships seem to be put into a more perfect order under God.

Recently I asked God for a specific ministry, not knowing what he'd give me. Two weeks later I was employed by the Christian Broadcasting Network as Houston Director of the 700 Club. I praise God for the exciting ways he is leading us and guiding us and loving us in every area of our lives. Jean and I are both involved in this ministry. The TV ministry of the 700 Club includes a panel of telephones for people to call during the nightly two-hour program for salvation, baptism with the Holy Spirit, healing, deliverance and other needs. One of our first acts was to pray, "Lord, we need 120 counselors per week within the next thirty days;" he gave them to us in seven days. We ministered salvation to about 124 people last month. Many people are healed every night in bodies, minds, marriages, finances and spiritual needs.

Would we go back? You know the answer to that. There's no way we could go back and receive less than what God has for us now. We praise God for the joy of our children. They still have some fusses once in a while, but in the Lord they're growing and maturing and receiving responsibility and gaining concepts from the teaching of the word and the fellowship of the believers and in Christian guidance in their home that I wish every child in America could have. It's God doing it, and we praise him for it! Why should "I" speak in tongues? It changed me and my family from death to life — new life in Christ Jesus — WITH POWER!

A. L. AND JOYCE GILL

"Through the baptism with the Holy Spirit, we have found, and are finding continuously, more of Jesus: MORE REALITY, MORE LOVE AND MORE POWER!"

"We are Christ's ambassadors." 2 Cor. 5:20 (TLB) The diplomat became an ambassador when he received his credentials and spoke in tongues!

A. L. and Joyce, like so many of us, changed quickly from the desert of a busy, sincere religious life to springs of living waters gushing from the Rock when Jesus baptized them with fire — with the Holy Spirit!

As we have ministered with them we have seen the freedom of the Spirit of God move through them. Their Christian maturity has been phenomenal since their baptism with the Holy Spirit. The book of Acts of the Gills containing the miracles of healing, salvation, deliverance, baptism and changing lives for Jesus would, if written, contain perhaps more than twenty-eight chapters.

Luke 11:36 (TLB) paints a picture of their faces filled with the joy of discipleship for Jesus: "If you are filled with light within, with no dark corners, then your face will be radiant too, as though a floodlight is beamed upon you."

A. L. Gill is Executive Vice-President of Hunter Ministries. He was formerly Administrative Assistant to Pastor Ralph Wilkerson at Melodyland Christian Center in Anaheim, California. Prior to that he was General Manager of the Western Berean Stores, a large chain of Christian bookstores in the western United States. A. L. also developed a major distribution center, representing most of the top evangelical publishers to all of the Christian bookstores in the southwest.

Joyce is now Office Manager of Hunter Ministries and is working in the area of publishing. She had also been involved for many years in Christian bookstore management and served as merchandise manager for the Berean Stores for a number of years.

The Gills have three children; John — 21, Kathy — 14, and Cindy — 9.

... "We dot our theological "i's" and cross our theological "t's"; but where is the power?"

... "Where is the reality of the person and power of Jesus in our lives. The power that we see in the lives of the early Christians in the book of Acts?"

... "THERE MUST BE MORE!!"

As I stood teaching the adult class in our church in Whittier, California, I challenged them, week after week, with these words. More than that, I was expressing a desire in my own life — a void deep within me — the lack of love and power in my life. I FELT THERE HAD TO BE MORE TO THE CHRISTIAN LIFE THAN WHAT I WAS EXPERIENCING IN MY OWN LIFE.

Could it be that there was something to this thing called the "baptism with the Holy Spirit"? I had been taught that this was a wild emotional experience, worked up by a group of Pentecostals who had not been "grounded in the word of God." It could even be of the devil, for these gifts of tongues, healings and miracles were just temporary spiritual gifts that stopped in the first century. I had heard about these people — all they could talk about was the "Holy Ghost" and they seldom mentioned Jesus. Certainly this did not line up with the word of God.

It was about this time that we began to notice a number of different people who were regular customers of the Christian bookstore that we managed. Every time they came in they talked about Jesus with a refreshing joy and enthusiasm. These were the people that Joyce and I really looked forward to seeing because they were always a blessing and a lift to our day. They were "a breath of fresh air." We could tell they had a vital, personal relationship with Jesus and when we had a prayer request, it was these individuals that we would ask to pray with us.

About this same time we were reading a number of books telling about the baptism in the Holy Spirit and we began to wonder if this was the difference that we felt in our friends. We began asking them, one by one, the next time that they came into the store, "Do you pray in tongues?", or "Do you have this thing called the baptism in the Holy Spirit?"

And just as we had suspected, THEY DID!

We began to study the scriptures and to read more books on the subject. We met several of the authors, Pat and Shirley Boone, George Otis and others who had this experience. Could this be, could this possibly be the "more" that we were looking for in our own lives?

We began to discuss this possibility with different people, and often the discussion would end with this phrase: "Look how the Lord is using Charles and Frances Hunter, and they don't have this 'thing.' " They were our "out."

Then we heard! CHARLES AND FRANCES HAD LET US DOWN. THEY HAD "GONE OFF INTO TONGUES!" Now we were convinced that this must be of God . . . but it was a special blessing that God had for some people! It probably wouldn't happen to us. Look how the Lord was using me in my job as General Manager of a chain of Christian bookstores, and as teacher of the adult class in my church. If this happened to me, I could lose my job and be asked to stop teaching, or even to leave the church.

We decided the next time the Hunters came to California we would have to find out for ourselves what this was all about. So we did. As we were sitting across the breakfast table from them, I finally got up enough courage to ask, "Ah . . . this baptism in the Holy Spirit . . . it's not for everyone, is it?"

"Yes, it's for everyone," Charles said. They shared what the baptism meant to them, and then went on talking about Jesus.

I said to Joyce as we left there, "If it ever happens to me, it would have to be in private . . . the shower, or someplace like that . . . because it wouldn't do for people to know that I had 'gone off into tongues.' " But that desire for more of Jesus continued to grow every day.

On September 24, 1972, early Sunday morning, we had started down from our mountain home at Big Bear Lake. As we rounded a curve on the mountain road we saw the most beautiful sunrise we have ever seen! As I pulled into a turnoff overlooking the lake, Doug Oldham began to sing *The King Is Coming* on the stereo in the car. We turned the stereo up, jumped from the car and stood there, spellbound by the reality of the soon coming of Jesus. As God unfolded a spectacular golden sunrise, we actually waited for the gates of heaven to open and for Jesus to appear. Could this be the day when Jesus would come? Our hearts raced with excitement! This was a day of new beginnings with Jesus for us, as this was the day when Jesus would baptize us with the Holy Spirit.

The week before, Charles and Frances had called on the telephone and invited us to come to Palm Springs where they would be speaking at the Full Gospel Business Men's Convention. "Well, ah, let me ask Joyce," and with my hand placed carefully over the receiver, I did.

"ARE YOU KIDDING? YOU KNOW WHAT GOES ON AT THOSE CONVENTIONS! " she whispered back.

I made some polite excuse. Then they said that they would also be speaking at Melodyland Christian Center on Sunday evening and we made arrangements to meet them there and to go out for something to eat afterwards.

We had been to Melodyland several years before for a David Wilkerson Rally, but as we walked into the church that evening I remember thinking that I'd better be careful who saw me there as it might not be good for business! Already Melodyland was known for its leadership in the Charismatic Movement. The church was nearly packed when we arrived, I got the Hunter's attention to let them know that we were there and would meet them afterwards, and we found seats in the back.

That night they gave their testimony of receiving Jesus as their Savior and then they began sharing their story of receiving the baptism with the Holy Spirit. Hundreds went into the prayer room afterwards. (I found out later that this prayer room used to be the largest bar in Orange County.)

As the service ended, we hurried to where the Hunters were, then in typical Hunter style we rushed to a small room where they shared briefly with a young married class on "How to make Your Marriage Exciting." Following that we stopped at the baptistry where a baptismal service was already in progress. A long line of people were waiting to be baptized; more people than I had ever seen baptized before. I found out later that this happened twice a week at Melodyland. As we stood there watching several being baptized, I noticed something very unusual; something that I had never seen before. As many came up out of the water they would raise their hands and begin praying in a strange language. I thought, "This must be the tongues that I have heard about." It was beautiful!

Then Frances said, "We've got to hurry to the prayer room."

As they started, Joyce squeezed my hand. NO WAY, NO WAY WERE WE GOING TO GO IN THERE! I told Frances and Charles that we would wait for them inside the auditorium. So we took a seat at the back of the auditorium and waited. I began to feel that desire for more of Jesus rising up inside of me, but I didn't mention it because I didn't want anyone to think I was getting caught up in all of this. A couple of times I got up and walked to where I could look in to see what was going on; once I even walked all the way into the prayer room and looked around. To my surprise they weren't shouting, or even waving their hands. They were sitting quietly and talking, or praying, with counselors, a scene I was familiar with having served as a counselor and later as an advisor with

Billy Graham Crusades. I went back to my seat and reported that everything seemed to be in order.

The Hunters came running out of the prayer room, apologizing for keeping us waiting. Frances was coming right toward me. By this time we were standing just inside the main door to Melodyland. Frances said, "A. L., the glory of the Lord is all over you!" (I had felt something but didn't know what it was.) "Are you ready?"

Joyce had often referred to me as "the diplomat," as I was known for my diplomacy, so she was thinking, "I wonder how he is going to get out of this one diplomatically."

At that moment, much to her surprise, I just raised my hands and said, "Zap me! "

Frances laid her hands on my head and prayed, "Jesus, baptize him with the Holy Spirit." At her instruction I opened my mouth and said a couple of syllables and then, suddenly, I was aware of the most beautiful language . . . a language that I had never heard before, pouring from my lips. I did not want to stop. I had my hands raised and people standing around could hear me, but I didn't care. It was real. I HAD NEVER FELT CLOSER TO THE LORD JESUS: IT WAS LIKE WAVES OF LOVE POURING THROUGH ME. I didn't want to stop because perhaps if I did, I couldn't start again. It was just Jesus and me. A miracle was taking place in my mouth, since these words were not coming from my mind or thoughts, but from deep within my spirit.

As Frances had begun to pray with me, and Joyce heard me praying in tongues, she felt I had betrayed her. Charles asked her if she too would like to receive. She said, "Charles, I don't even know what you are talking about! " He explained briefly, then prayed with her and she too received the infilling of the Holy Spirit.

Later, driving to the motel with the Hunters, they told us that we might not think that there was much difference at first, but that we would notice there was more love in our lives. People would begin to ask us what was different about us; and that we would begin to notice more power in our prayers. THAT IS EXACTLY WHAT HAPPENED!

Immediately we felt a love for the Lord Jesus that was more real. He was close! We had more love for his word. It seemed we couldn't spend enough time with him in prayer and in reading his Bible. Our hearts were full of love and praise for the Lord. We soon ran out of words in English with which to express the praise that we felt, but now we could shift into our new langauge and continue to praise him. I believe this language is the "tongues of angels" spoken of in I Corinthians.

At first Joyce did not have an easy flow and freedom in this new language, but as she continued to praise God in the few words she had, God gave her more and more, until she too had a beautiful flow in her new tongue.

In addition to the new love that we felt for the Lord Jesus, we also noticed that we had more love and concern for our family, our friends and others.

We did not share our experience with anyone at first. We could remember how we had been turned off by people in the past who had been too forceful with us. We wanted to wait and then to speak in God's timing. Then one by one, people began to ask, "What is the difference?" We found that many of our friends had been experiencing the same desire that we had felt for more of the reality of the person and power of Jesus in their lives. We had the privilege of sharing with them what the "more" was and of praying for many of our friends and family to receive the infilling of the Holy Spirit.

Frances and Charles had mentioned also that there would be more power in our lives. I wasn't sure what that meant. I knew that the love and reality of the presence of Jesus was the most important thing in our lives. Then it happened! Several weeks after we had received the baptism with the Holy Spirit, we were at our place at Big Bear Lake for the weekend. We had been hanging draperies all evening and Joyce suddenly realized a vertebrae in her neck was out of place and that she was developing a terrible headache. I stood behind her massaging her neck for a minute and then, without thinking, I prayed silently. All at once Joyce spun around and asked, "Did you pray?"

She said, "I felt two hands pulling the spine back into place." THE PAIN WAS COMPLETELY GONE! Her first reaction had been trying to figure out how I had done it, and then the realization hit that the hands were on the inside!

Our teenage son, John, was sitting on a stool across the room watching the whole thing take place. He held up his finger and said, "Dad, what about my finger?" John had hurt his finger on a rock-hounding trip the week before. We had determined that probably it was not broken and told him to watch it closely and, if needed, we would take him to the doctor. Here it was, the following week and we had forgotten to ask him about the finger all week! He was holding the finger toward me. It had swollen to twice the normal size and was black and blue. He could move it only slightly.

After examining the finger I asked him, "John, do you believe God can heal your finger?"

"Yes."

"Do you believe he wants to heal it now?"

Yes!" he replied again.

"Then let's just ask him to do it." I took his finger and enclosed it gently in my hand and prayed simply, "Jesus touch him." I opened my hand and looked. The finger had returned to normal size and the discoloration was completely gone. He could bend it with no pain. God had healed that finger!

Our daughter Kathy ran over to see! As John held out both hands, he asked Kathy which finger was hurt. She picked the finger on the wrong hand! Then we remembered what Charles had said about more power.

From this time on almost everywhere we went miracles were taking place. More and more people were coming to us and asking for prayer. Now we truly believed in the power of prayer and now God began to heal: deaf ears opened, burns disappeared, people walked out of wheel chairs, and left their crutches. One young boy walked for the first time in his life. Short legs and arms have grown out and people have been instantly delivered from arthritis. Hundreds have fallen under the power of God! We cannot begin to remember all of the fantastic miracles we have seen.

Perhaps no one has been more astonished in all of this than Joyce and I, for we know that we have absolutely nothing to do with it. We certainly have no healing power. It is only the power of the Holy Spirit flowing through us. It is the river of living water, flowing from our innermost beings. Before we received the baptism we had felt a measure of the fullness of the Holy Spirit many times, but now it is flowing like an artesian well . . . not blessing only us but many around us.

We don't want people to think that our lives have been a continuous mountain-top experience since receiving the baptism. There have been many valleys, deep valleys of trials and testings. But it has been in those valleys that we really have learned to know the Lord Jesus in a special way. It is in the valleys that we have found what the victorious Christian life is all about. The baptism with the Holy Spirit didn't mean that our problems would be gone. It meant we now had the power to find the victory through our problems. On many occasions we have not known how to pray about the situation we were in, so we have learned to pray in our prayer language . . . letting the Holy Spirit do the interceding.

One of the greatest privileges has been in ministering

with Charles and Frances Hunter in their miracle services. Last winter we went to San Diego to join the Hunters for two days of services there and then to Escondido for two more days. The second morning, which was Saturday, we were busy getting ready for a service when I asked Joyce where my thyroid pills were. I had been taking thyroid for fifteen years. Joyce hadn't packed them! I almost panicked! Immediately I began to plan: as soon as I drive the Hunters to the church, I'll drive back to Los Angeles and get the pills. That was a four hour trip. Perhaps I can take the group over to the church and then see if I can find a druggist who would call my pharmacist in Whittier and get the prescription, or perhaps . . . Joyce interrupted my thoughts.

"Do you believe God can heal your thyroid condition?"

How could she bother me at a time like this. I had to make a quick decision.

"Do you believe God wants to heal your thyroid condition?" Second question!

"Yes, of course . . . " But I remembered the Saturday a couple of years before when I had tried to believe God for my thyroid healing. I had prayed about it when I got up that morning and then had not taken the thyroid. By the middle of the afternoon I was dizzy and seeing double. I gave in and took the medicine. This weekend in San Diego and Escondido was certainly not the time to be "out of it."

"Do you believe that God wants to heal your thyroid?" Joyce interrupted again!

If I could only know, but this just was not the time to risk it. But . . . it did seem strange to miss a service where I was to pray with the sick in order to go and get my own medicine.

Then I thought of how I had prayed before I left the house for the Lord to remind me if I had forgotten anything that I would need. Then as we were leaving the house, Joyce felt impressed to go back into the house, and she had prayed in each room asking the Lord if anything was forgotten. The Lord had showed her one thing, then she felt release and came back to the car. I couldn't remember ever having done this so definitely before. Surely he would have reminded one of us of the thyroid — if I really needed it. Could it be that he really was going to heal me?

"A. L., DO YOU BELIEVE THAT GOD CAN HEAL YOU?"

"YES! I KNOW HE CAN! "

Joyce prayed and I fell back across the bed under the power of God and I believed that God had healed me!

We had a powerful service that morning! But as we were getting ready for the evening service, I remembered my thyroid. The drug stores would be closing in a few minutes and the next day was Sunday. In that moment of doubt all the symptoms hit me. I was ready to run for a drug store. Again we prayed and again the Lord gave me the faith to believe him for healing. The symptoms left and we went on to have an absolutely fabulous miracle service both that Saturday and all day Sunday and Monday.

On Tuesday morning I was in the bathroom in our motel in Escondido. We were preparing to take the Hunters back to San Diego to catch a plane and from there we were going home. Suddenly the thought hit me, "You have not needed your thyroid here, but as soon as you get home where you have your supply you will need it again."

I said, "Satan, I rebuke you and I rebuke that negative thought in the name of Jesus. I do not accept that! "

At that moment Joyce walked into the room and said, "Guess what the devil just told me?"

"I know," I said, "because he just tried to tell me the same thing."

She had not wanted to tell me, for she also had recognized the source of that thought and had not wanted to pass it on to me, but the Lord had impressed her to tell me. We laughed together at the devil and told him that he was a liar and to "get lost! " That evening at home I destroyed the remainder of the prescription. The healing is total and complete as I write this, nine months later.

One of the things the Lord has shown us in the past three years is that a miracle is very personal. It is hard to explain to another what the Lord has done for you. So I have asked Joyce to write in her own words concerning the healing of her eyes.

Joyce

Soon after we received the baptism with the Holy Spirit, I broke the frames of my glasses. We were in a hurry getting ready to meet the Hunters at the airport, so I grabbed some nylon thread and tied them together. "Someday Lord," I thought, "I'll not need these anymore!" That thread was to last about two years.

Time after time, in various meetings, the word of knowledge came for eye healings and I placed my hands on my eyes. Others prayed for me but nothing happened.

I have worn glasses for 24 years and it was not unusual for A. L. to remind me to take them off as I was falling asleep at night. In the morning my first move was that of my hand feeling the night stand in the dark for them. If I didn't find them quickly, someone in the family looked for them for me as I would get an almost instant headache. I could see clearly for about four feet and then everything appeared blurred.

Recently, while in the mountains for a weekend, we and a friend had spent almost the entire Saturday praying and studying the Bible. We had no "project" in mind; God kept calling us to prayer. As the house settled for the night and the three of us were still praying, God told A. L. and Pat to pray for my eyes.

"Why not," I responded, and took off my glasses.

They prayed as the Lord led for about twenty minutes, until I felt a popping to the side of my eyes and began to look around. I could read a plaque hanging across the room! We went from room to room seeing what I could see!

I didn't want to go to sleep but, of course, I did in time. We were up again at five the next morning, as I couldn't wait any longer. I had to see what I could see in the daylight. I stood on the deck and saw individual trees across the lake on the opposite mountain! I didn't know what normal eyesight was, so all day Sunday I was checking my sight by everyone. Could they see this? How clearly did they see that? It was exciting!

But at times I could see almost nothing! Instantly someone would reject Satan's attack and my clear vision returned. By three Sunday afternoon I was exhausted from the lack of sleep, the continuous checking, the battle with Satan and the feeling I wasn't completely dressed. Wearing those glasses was a habit! My hands searched for them even as I was praising God for his healing.

The three of us went to prayer again and I asked the Father how long this battle would go on. He replied, "Until my word becomes concrete within your heart."

Then I asked the Lord for a definite verse to become "concrete within." I needed a positive verse from him. He gave us the reference, Isaiah 60:4: LIFT UP YOUR EYES AND SEE, from the Living Bible. For the next week I claimed this verse out loud every time my vision became clouded. Many times this was more an act of obedience of the will than one of high faith.

About Thursday of that week, I remember I told the Lord that if he had chosen this time to heal my eyes because of my strong faith, he had made a mistake! But if it were a gift of his love, great! I accept it!

The following Sunday I was over the feeling of having forgotten something. My hands no longer felt continuously for the glasses as I thought of something else. The waves of poor vision were almost past, but I still couldn't see clearly in the fluorescent lights of the supermarket.

The second Monday morning I knew it was time to go to the Department of Motor Vehicles and get the corrective lens restriction removed from my driver's license. It had been years ago that I had discovered I needed glasses when I first applied for my driver's license. THEY WOULDN'T GIVE ME A LICENSE WITHOUT GLASSES! I was certain that the office would be brightly lighted with fluorescent lights, and they were still bothering me. I could see just great as I drove to the D.M.V. office but when I walked into the office with the fluorescent lighting, EVERYTHING BLURRED! I walked over to where the eye charts were and I couldn't see them!

"Lord, what am I doing here?"

I walked up to the first window and told the lady that I wanted to get the restriction removed from my driver's license. She told me to go to Window 27, so I went to that line and took my place. I could see nothing.

"Lord, I have to see that chart!"

I was third in line. Everything was blurred.

I was second in line. Everything was blurred.

I was next . . . EVERYTHING WAS BLURRED!

"Father, this is the last minute! If you're not in this, it is the most stupid thing I have ever done!"

It was my turn and everything was still blurred, but I walked up to the window and told the man I would like to get the corrective-lens restriction removed. He told me to step over to the machine. (I didn't have to read the chart hanging under the fluorescent light.) I read all three charts in the machine down to the second from the last number. I PASSED!

The girl who typed my temporary license asked what had happened and I told her that God had healed me. She rejoiced with me. I returned to Window 27 and took my place in line again, but this time in peace. It was a different man this time, and he asked if I had contacts on.

"No."

"Did you have an operation?" He was staring intently at my eyes.

"No, God healed my eyes."

"WHAT?"

"God healed my eyes."

"Get over to that machine," he demanded. I had to take the test over. This time I read all three charts — rapidly — down to the very last number!

Driving home I was rejoicing out loud. "God, I can see! I can really see without those glasses. You have healed me! Isn't that great, you have really healed me!"

So often with me, it is like God and I share a laugh together and this day was no exception for suddenly, as I was rejoicing out loud, I heard my Father say in a very dry voice, "You were healed a week ago."

Now, I knew I had been!

We could go on for hours describing what the Lord has done since we received the baptism in the Holy Spirit. Sometimes it is easier to tell of miracles, and as we write we rejoice over them again, but the real difference in our lives goes much deeper. There is no way to explain to another how we have changed completely. God has become "my Father" in reality. Jesus, a very close friend and Savior, and the power of the Holy Spirit flows out to others at any time, day or night. We live a new, exciting life. Often it is very joyful; other times the joy is almost hidden by the tears, but always our Father is there. THROUGH THE BAPTISM WITH THE HOLY SPIRIT WE HAVE FOUND, AND ARE FINDING CONTINUOUSLY, MORE OF JESUS: MORE REALITY, MORE LOVE, AND MORE POWER.

JERRY WOODFILL
NASA Space Engineer,
Johnson Space Center
Houston, Texas

"I knew that any subject or thing that drew so many people so suddenly must be from Jesus! The longer I spoke (in tongues) the closer I felt to Christ and the more assurance I received of his reality and love."

"Then he was filled with the joy of the Holy Spirit and said, 'I praise you, O Father, Lord of heaven and earth, for hiding these things from the intellectuals and worldly wise and for revealing them to those who are as trusting as little children. Yes, thank you, Father, for that is the way you wanted it.' " Luke 10:21 (TLB)

Intellectual Jerry Woodfill looked beyond his boundaries as the worldly wise, and discovered that when he bypassed his intellect and by faith allowed his spirit to talk to God in an unknown tongue, he pleased God because that is the way God wanted it.

The Holy Spirit is so mightily being poured out on all flesh that people in high places, the socially elite, the leaders of business, government and military are coming as trusting as little children, lifting their hands to God in surrender and praising God and speaking in other tongues as the Spirit gives them utterance.

Jerry Woodfill is a NASA Space Engineer at the Johnson Space Center in Houston, Texas. His career there has included development and management of the Apollo Caution and Warning Systems of the Command and Lunar Module spacecraft. During the Apollo 13 Mission when the spacecraft exploded nearly 200,000 miles from earth, Jerry served as part of the mission operations team which successfully rescued the crew of astronauts. As part of this effort as member of this JSC team, he received the Presidential Medal of Freedom. Presently he serves NASA as a Technical Monitor and Project Engineer of the Earth Resources Program.

In 1972, Jerry found Christ as his Savior and Lord at a Full Gospel Businessmen's breakfast in a Houston motel. Several weeks later, he received the baptism of the Holy Spirit at the home of Charles and Frances Hunter. Presently he serves his United Methodist Church as Missions Chairman and as Church School Instructor.

Recently, Jerry participated in the Full Gospel Businessmen's retreat and airlift to Belize, Central America. Many leaders of the country of Belize received Christ as Savior and Baptizer on this crusade.

Attending Rice University on a basketball athletic scholarship, Jerry played in varsity competition throughout the United States. He graduated from Rice in 1965 with BSEE and BAEE degrees prior to joining NASA. He is local director of the Houston Chapter of the Full Gospel Businessmen's Fellowship International and he is also a trustee of the Hunter Foundation and a member of the Texas Society of Professional Engineers.

Betty and I were part of a small Bible study on Colossians the Hunters had been holding in their home for several months. Although it was a very long drive for us on a weekday evening (40 miles), both of us were drawn to the joy in Christ which we found each week in their home. . . sharing and studying.

During the closing of the first meeting while in a prayer circle, Charles suddenly began to pray that all there would receive the infilling of the Holy Spirit. After praying, he shared with us that he felt most of us would receive the baptism of the Holy Spirit. This was confusing to me for I HAD NEVER HEARD MENTION OF AN INFILLING OR BAPTISM OF THE HOLY SPIRIT IN MY ENTIRE EXPERIENCE. I had been a member of Lutheran and Methodist churches and active as Sunday school superintendent, board member, etc.

We continued to study Colossians and in the interim a friend invited me to attend a Full Gospel Businessmen's breakfast in Houston where I was overcome by the presence of the Holy Spirit and went forward to give my life to Christ. They spoke also of this experience but I remained confused and determined to ask the Hunters more about this.

Shortly afterward when we were leaving the meeting I asked Charles to teach me what this experience was all about. I was confused, especially about the experience of speaking in tongues. Charles shared with me that at this point we might have a kind of aftermeeting or for me to come by his home some evening and we could talk at length.

A few weeks later while I was mowing the grass, Betty called me to stop and come to the phone to talk with Frances. She invited me to come to their home for a special meeting on the baptism of the Holy Spirit, and to bring my guitar. We had a house guest, my sister, but I was determined to go and we brought her with us that evening.

When we arrived I was completely surprised by the presence of so many people. We remembered how during that past Christmas season attendance had been so few that we were feeling bad because more people weren't coming to enjoy the study. I could hardly believe it but there were 70 people crammed into the living and dining rooms and there was no place for me to sit but on the floor to play the guitar. I KNEW THAT ANY SUBJECT OR THING THAT DREW SO MANY PEOPLE SO SUDDENLY MUST BE FROM JESUS!

What came next probably did more than anything to sell me on the importance of this experience. Charles and Frances shared their testimony of how it had changed their lives to become even greater witnesses for Jesus. They shared that it would give each of us much greater power through the Holy Spirit to win others to him. They explained about the experience of speaking in tongues, which comes as evidence of the baptism, and how they received this. Charles asked those men who desired to receive to remain in the living room and for the ladies who wanted to receive to go with Frances. I stayed in the living room and Betty went to the rear with Frances.

Charles gathered us in a circle and we began to pray, expecting the Holy Spirit to fall on us. Just at that moment the phone rang and Charles was called from the room to minister to a person in need in a distant city. I thought, "What now, Lord? You've taken Charles away and I was counting on having him pray with me."

There were several Spirit-filled people in the room who had been invited to help minister and I asked them to pray with me. I knelt down and they placed their hands gently upon me and prayed for Jesus to baptize me with the Holy Spirit. Not much happened except that three words came to my mind which I gave utterance to over and over. They were three Latin words which I recognized as,

"Glory to God, who we love." This was quite remarkable since I never could speak Latin and could hardly translate it in its written form. About this time, I suddenly heard a very guttural language, very loud and interspersed with tears and groans and crying out. I looked up and there was a good friend of mine from my Methodist Church near NASA speaking an entire language with his hands uplifted and tears streaming down his face. I really felt envious and thought, "Lord, how come him and not me? I'm certainly just as worthy, and I've got only three words from you . . . not a language." I didn't remember that Jesus isn't concerned with our works but looks on our faith and the condition of our hearts.

Charles returned and I felt, "Well maybe that's all I'm ever going to get with this baptism. I certainly don't have a whole language though." It was late and more prayer was given for others. I packed up my guitar, and Betty came from the back, having received with a whole language in another tongue and we were preparing to leave.

Frances asked at the door, "Jerry, do you really love Jesus?" I replied, "I really love him more than anything." I lifted my hands to him and really was feeling his love for me when Frances gently placed her hands just under my chin. Suddenly I started to speak a whole string of words and phrases which seemed to come up through me just as water flowing out of a well pump with my mouth as the spigot. It was wonderful . . . so free and flowing and I could start and stop at will! It was a miracle! I thought to myself, "This is indeed a miracle like a healing from the Holy Spirit! Praise the Lord!"

I drove home with Betty and it was late when we got to bed. I was so happy and thankful for Jesus giving me a miracle in my life. I just laid there in bed thinking of how wonderful he was to baptize me with the Holy Spirit.

Suddenly the thought came, "I might not be able to speak this new language ever again or at best when I felt very close to the Lord."

I looked at Betty and she was asleep. I didn't want to wake her and thought she might think it silly for me if I spoke in tongues and awakened her. I quietly slipped out of bed and into the den and laid down on the sofa and raised my hands. THERE IT WAS HAPPENING AGAIN! I could even drop my hands and speak this language. I could speed up to a very high word rate per minute or slow down to a snail's pace with this new language. I started to listen to myself and heard certain key words like "Colia" which seemed to be repeated in key spots of the sentences I spoke. It was like having a new automobile and trying it out on the road. The longer I spoke the closer I felt to Christ and the more assurance I received of his reality and love for me in that room. The next morning I tested the language at greater length. I found that I would speak a series of words, sometimes as many as twenty-five, and could repeat the entire series without missing a syllable. I didn't even have to make an effort to memorize the entire passage. I spent much time later testing and marveling in the miraculous nature of this gift from Christ.

I studied Paul's comments in depth and they entirely confirmed my experience. As I would start to praise God, and sing and speak in this heavenly language, I often would start to weep! Then I'd begin to sing in the Spirit and the melody would come along with the words. Later I began to speak entire sermons to myself in the car, without any attempt to prepare the text or material. Finally, as I spoke in the tongue he had given me, I began to receive entire prophesies given to me from Christ for encouragement, correction, and edification. The depth of my experience in Christ greatly increased as I communed with him in this new way, and many times a day I would participate in this worship.

I still continue to pray and worship in this way to the extent that IT IS AS NATURAL TO ME AS SPEAKING TO MY

CHILDREN OR WIFE.

Not long ago, I was asleep and dreaming that I was laying my hands on a person to receive this experience from Christ. I awoke speaking in this unknown language. It has served to fill my entire being with Jesus Christ.

I have found that speaking in tongues is a powerful tool from God for the Spirit-filled Christian. In my life there have been five major areas where this gift has been most effective.

The first way has been in increasing my faith and assurance that Jesus lives in me and loves me. Speaking in tongues has been a guarantee of the presence of his Spirit in me and with me. Prior to receiving a heavenly language, I was too shy to witness my faith in Christ. Afterwards, I began to share with everyone, including people in airplanes, taxi drivers, a bell hop, engineers and scientists with NASA. In my office, I have prayed with two space technologists to receive Christ as Savior and Lord, not fearing what people would think of me. I found new boldness through use of this supernatural ability from the Holy Spirit and found myself on one commercial flight asking the stewardess if I might visit the crew. Later she took me forward and I shared my faith with them as they piloted the jet aircraft at 35,000 feet. Usually prior to visiting or witnessing I pray in tongues and the Lord gives me strength and assurance as he did when I shared with these pilots.

The second area has been the leading I received from the Holy Spirit as a result of praying in tongues. Remarkable opportunities to share my faith with people occur. On occasion I have received phone calls just as I ceased praying in tongues from individuals needing prayer or help. I began to be led to people who were open to receiving Christ when there was no apparent clue other than the leading of the Holy Spirit. One man called me who I had never met needing financial and medical help. We prayed together and that week he received $4,500! Since then he has made over $200,000 and his health and life have been restored. He has become a born-again Spirit-filled Christian who speaks in tongues also.

The third way that speaking in tongues has profited my life in Christ has been through guiding me in my intercessions for myself and others. Many times I haven't understood how to pray for a need or what to pray. In my uncertainty, I pray in the Spirit, knowing that the perfect prayer and intercession is being made to God by the Holy Spirit through me. As an example, I was rooming with a high government official of a foreign country. He was an agnostic and closed to discussion of Christ and belief in him. While he was away from our room, I placed my hands on his pillow and prayed in tongues for several minutes. About a month later I received a letter from him. He had turned to Christ and accepted him. Guess where? IN HIS BED!

The fourth work of speaking in tongues has been as a spiritual weapon of great power against the enemy, Satan. Often the devil will come against me and try to scare, defeat or discourage me in my Christian walk. When I face these battles, I pray in tongues in order that the Holy Spirit can defeat him and Christ will win the victory. Before having this gift to speak in tongues it frightened me to do combat with Satan. I avoided encounters and backed away from the battle. When people were oppressed by Satan in some way I often avoided praying with them. Through this gift I have become bold in facing the enemy knowing that the Holy Spirit will win the battle. A Christian friend of ours had been staying in the home of a person involved in spiritism and the occult. As a result, ugly sores appeared on her forearm which did not heal or respond to treatment. She mentioned this and I found in me the faith and boldness in Christ to lay my hand on the sores and command Satan to be bound and for the sores to depart in Jesus' name. They disappeared in the next 48 hours. Prior to speaking in tongues I would have retreated from such a situation.

Lastly, the ability from the Holy Spirit to speak in tongues has helped me to minister the baptism of the Holy Spirit to others so that they also can have this wonderful gift from God. Shortly after receiving this gift, Charles asked me to pray for a young man at his home to receive the baptism of the Holy Spirit. At the time I was uncertain if I should or could pray for another to receive. I didn't want to disappoint my friend Charles, so I placed my hands on him and as I started to pray in the Spirit, he burst forth also with an entire unknown language different from mine.

I found that I could minister this gift to others as Peter and Paul had. I have seen Baptist Sunday school teachers and businessmen, Methodist scientists, Disciple of Christ housewives, the young and old, receive the baptism of the Holy Spirit and speak in a fluent unknown language as I prayed for them to receive just as I was prayed for by Frances in their den near 12 midnight. They who have received this gift rejoice as I did in witnessing a miracle gift from Christ flow from their lips. It is wonderful to know that he dwells in me and uses my body to serve him through this miracle of speaking in tongues.

It has proved to be the most powerful weapon and tool which he has given me to reach others for Christ! It has made the scripture, "We are more than conquerers through him," an everyday reality in my life for him.

DR. AND MRS.
STEPHEN P. GYLAND

"When we found out that the same baptism in the Holy Spirit was available for Christians today, WE WANTED IT . . . WE GOT IT . . . AND WE WERE TRANSFORMED INSTANTLY!"

TWENTY-FIVE YEARS AFTER THE DAY OF PENTECOST: "While Apollos was in Corinth, Paul traveled through Turkey and arrived in Ephesus, where he found several disciples. 'Did you receive the Holy Spirit when you believed?' he asked them. 'No,' they replied, 'we don't know what you mean. What is the Holy Spirit?' " Acts 19:1-2 (TLB) "Then, when Paul laid his hands upon their heads, the Holy Spirit came on them, and they spoke in other languages and prophesied." Acts 19:6 (TLB)

"My wife, Rose, and I had been Christians most of our lives, but Jesus had been almost last in our affections . . . TWENTY-FIVE YEARS . . . The next part of the teaching was *equally astounding because we heard much teaching about the baptism in the Holy Spirit.*"

Steve and Rose discovered that TWENTY-FIVE YEARS after the Day of Pentecost people were still receiving the baptism and speaking in tongues — the procedure and manifestation was not changed. They had spent twenty-five years in Christianity when they first heard similar questions to the one Paul asked: "Did you receive the Holy Spirit when you believed?" Steve and Rose replied, "No, we don't know what you mean. What is the Holy Spirit?" . . . Brothers in Christ laid hands upon them and the Holy Spirit came on them and they spoke in other languages — just like on the Day of Pentecost.

Stephen
Graduate of Vanderbilt Medical School
BS in Chemistry, MD
Phi Beta Kappa, AOA
Pediatric Residency at Tulane University, New Orleans
Private practice of Pediatrics
Secretary of the Florida Pediatric Association
Former Chairman of the Mayor's Health Advisory Board of Jacksonville

Rose
BS in Bacteriology at the University of North Carolina
Certified teacher in Florida for Marine Biology, Chemistry and Biology
Working toward Master of Divinity in Religious Education

Both of them are certified scuba divers and accomplished yachtsmen and have cruised extensively in the Bahamas for several years.

DR. STEPHEN P. AND ROSE GYLAND

My wife, Rose, and I had been Christians most of our lives, but Jesus had been almost last in our affections. We had put the house, the medical practice, the children, social prestige, money, etc. ahead of the Lord Jesus Christ. One day about four years ago we found that several of our kids were on drugs and doing other wicked things. Although a successful doctor, I gradually had started drinking an ever-increasing amount of whiskey. Strangely enough, my wife had developed a very irritable disposition! Finally, as our marriage hit rock bottom and my wife told me that she was seeing her lawyer the next day and that I should see my lawyer, there "happened" to be a conference on family life with David DuPlessis, sponsored by the Full Gospel Business Men's Fellowship and St. Peter's Episcopal Church of Jacksonville. She took me to this to get me straightened out, and both she and I thought somebody had rewritten the Bible because the first thing we saw presented in the Bible was that wives should submit to their husbands. In twenty-five years this thought never had entered her mind, nor did I know it was scriptural!

The next part of the teaching was equally astounding because we heard much teaching about the baptism in the Holy Spirit. As Presbyterians we knew that the baptism in the Holy Spirit happened on the Day of Pentecost, but we thought it was a one-time deal like the crucifixion of our Lord Jesus Christ was a one-time deal. We found out that the crucifixion totally finished and perfected God's perfect plan of salvation, but the baptism in the Holy Spirit is recorded NOT JUST ON THE DAY OF PENTECOST BUT FOUR ADDITIONAL TIMES IN THE BOOK OF ACTS. After Philip preached Christ in Samaria, the apostles laid hands on these Samaritans who had received salvation and baptism in the water under Philip the evangelist. Why? So that they might receive the Holy Ghost.

Similarly, Paul on the road to Damascus saw the bright

light and became an "instant" Christian, but Ananias had to risk his very life to lay hands on Paul that he might be filled with the Holy Ghost. Also, at the house of Cornelius, the people RECEIVED SALVATION AND THE BAPTISM IN THE HOLY SPIRIT, this time simultaneously, or in close succession.

When Philip went down to the city of Ephesus and found certain disciples, he said, "Have ye received the Holy Ghost since ye believed?" Paul laid his hands upon them, and the HOLY SPIRIT CAME UPON THEM, AND THEY SPAKE WITH TONGUES AND PROPHESIED!

When we found out that the same baptism in the Holy Spirit was available for Christians today, we wanted it. We had tried running our lives our way and had made a total mess of everything. Now, we determined to live our lives the way of Jesus.

THINGS COULDN'T BE ANY WORSE ANYWAY.

We gave our lives completely to Jesus and asked him to give us what he had for us. We knelt and prayed, and because Jesus is the same yesterday and today and forever, he baptized us in the Holy Spirit just like on the Day of Pentecost. Brothers in Christ laid hands on us, and we received the baptism in the Holy Spirit and spoke a new language.

WE WERE TRANSFORMED INSTANTLY!

We had a SUPERNATURAL love pour out of us for all Christians and for everybody else, which has been undiminished in three and a half years. We had a SUPERNATURAL joy, so it was hard not to be singing and praising the Lord all the time. We had a SUPERNATURAL faith, so that although our three kids were still taking drugs we didn't worry one more minute, for the scripture says, "Cast all your cares upon him, for he cares for you." We were at this point able to do exactly that, and sure enough once you pray in faith, Jesus will answer your prayers. Within three months all three kids gave their lives to the

Lord Jesus Christ, and all three received the baptism in the Holy Spirit and spoke a new langauge. Since then our other three kids have received the baptism in the Holy Spirit. Hallelujah!

The day following the baptism in the Holy Spirit, I was treating a doctor's two-year-old child who was critically ill with spinal meningitis. My wife came down to the hospital to bring them some Christian literature to read. Then she smiled up at me.

She said, "May I touch the baby?"

I said, "Go ahead, but wash your hands afterward, because it's contagious."

She laid hands on the baby and prayed, although we hadn't read enough of the Bible yet to know that we were supposed to do this. WITHIN AN HOUR THE BABY WAS OUT OF DANGER AND SURVIVED WITHOUT ANY COMPLICATIONS.

Our life has been filled with miracles. We've not had one minute of unhappiness since that time. We've found that when we share Jesus a very few words frequently will lead someone to accept Jesus as his or her Savior and get born again, because IT'S NOT OUR WORDS ANY MORE BUT THE POWER OF THE HOLY SPIRIT.

We also find that a very few words will occasionally offend people. If they happen to be my patients, they'll change doctors. Here again, it's not my words but the power of the Holy Spirit, who shall convict the world of sin.

The miracles have continued to flood: cancer being healed, deaf ears opened, Meniere's syndrome healed. One of the exciting ones was when a lawyer came to our house who had not been a believer for thirty years. We asked him if we could pray for him at prayer meeting.

He said, "It wouldn't do any good, because I haven't believed anything you've said all night. I don't believe in Jesus, and I haven't prayed in thirty years."

I said to him, "Charlie, you need to see a miracle."

I asked if anybody in the room had back trouble caused by one leg being shorter than the other, because the visible miracle of a short leg growing out before people's very eyes convinces many that Jesus is exactly who he said he was, and that he is alive today and doing well. It's beautiful when cancer or leukemia or hemorrhoids get healed, but nobody can see these miracles! When a crippled limb straightens or a short leg grows out, this is what Larry Hammond calls the "Doubting Thomas" miracle. No Christian in the room had this.

Finally Charlie said, "Doctor, I do."

I thought of Jesus and his miracle-working ministry when he said, "Be it unto you according to your faith." Then, the Holy Spirit quickened Mark's gospel where Jesus said, "These signs shall follow them that believe.... They shall speak with new tongues ... they shall lay hands on the sick and they shall recover."

I said, "Lord, I'm a believer, and Charlie needs a sign, because the sign is for the unbeliever."

So I laid hands on Charlie in the name of Jesus and prayed for our Lord to show him a sign. His crippled leg grew out two or three inches in front of everybody's eyes, and Charlie's back was healed, his knees were healed, he could touch his toes, and he could kneel down for the first time in twenty years.

As he started to leave the prayer meeting an hour later with this same dazed expression on his face, I said, "Charlie, will you accept Jesus now?"

He said, "We'll wait and see if I'm still healed in the morning."

On the way home he stopped at the bar, and his testimony at the bar led another young man to accept Jesus! The next morning he had to buy new shoes, because the shoe with the built-up sole wouldn't fit anymore. He went back to Mexico where he was living in retirement and started preaching Jesus. The Lord took away his cigarettes and alcohol and straightened out the rest of his life. Paul said in the second chapter of First Corinthians that he did not come with enticing words of man's wisdom but in the demonstration of the power of the Holy Spirit. Hallelujah!

One night as we stood in our home prayer meeting, the Holy Spirit spoke in my wife's ears with an audible voice for the first time and said, "You need to forgive the drug pusher!" A certain drug pusher had gotten our kids started on drugs at an early age. We hadn't thought of this man in months! He was the only person who had been forbidden to ever come to our house. My wife, with a flood of tears and the power of God upon her, managed to forgive this drug pusher in open family prayer. Then my seventeen-year-old son said, "Thank you, Jesus. All day I've been praying and fasting for Mother to forgive the pusher," because he had been witnessing to him about Jesus. The next week at our family prayer meeting, the drug pusher came and we welcomed him with obvious love, which is the fruit of the Holy Spirit. We loved him and preached Jesus to him. Before the night was over he accepted Jesus as his Savior. Then he asked if he could receive the baptism with the Holy Spirit. We prayed with him and laid hands on him, and the power of God fell on this man and he spoke a new language and was transformed. How like our Lord Jesus! THE FIRST PERSON TO RECEIVE SALVATION AND TO RECEIVE THE PRECIOUS HOLY SPIRIT HAD BEEN THE ONLY HUMAN BEING EVER FORBIDDEN TO COME TO OUR HOME.

The next day this man was at the high school, Bible in his hand, fasting and praying and preaching Jesus. Hallelujah!

BOB MURPHY

"I have found one peculiarity in having the baptism with the Holy Spirit! When I formerly was drunk with alcohol, those who didn't drink looked down on me. Now that I'm drunk on the 'new wine' I've discovered that those who don't imbibe at the fountain of living water don't appreciate me either. Hallelujah!"

"And be not drunk with wine, wherein is excess; but be filled with the Spirit; Speaking to yourselves in psalms and hymns and spiritual songs, singing and making melody in your heart to the Lord." Ephesians 5:18-19 KJV

Bob Murphy is someone who switched from one fountain to the other and who found life in Jesus Christ! He attended Southwestern University in Georgetown, Texas, then fell into the bottle and spent many years as an alcoholic while playing, singing and talking at places like the Randolph Square Theatre Bar in Chicago, The Golden Horseshoe in Lexington, Kentucky, The House of Steele in Lake Bluff, Illinois, and many others.

Today he is the operator of Serenity Farm in Houston, Texas, a haven for alcoholics where he shares very simply what Jesus has done in his life. Today he still plays the organ with the same zeal he formerly did, but now he plays psalms and hymns and spiritual songs! Hallelujah! He is author of the book CHRISTIANITY RUBS HOLES IN MY RELIGION, published by Hunter Ministries Publishing Company.

In order to understand some of the experiences of my later life you must know something of my early life. I was born into a family of sincere fundamentalists and a religion which put great emphasis on negatives. In order to be "saved" one went down front at a public meeting, and with great emotion repented of his sins and accepted Jesus Christ as his Savior. One then began an impossible program of do-it-yourself perfection by giving up various habits and activities which were considered by the fundamentalists to be sinful.

Great emphasis was placed upon exterior trappings, how we looked, what we wore, where we went, and what we said or did not say. All this was presented as the "truth" which Christ said would set us free. I tried desperately to become a part of this religion but I did not find it truth for me. I certainly found no freedom.

So I decided at an early age that Christianity was a hopeless chore and a definite bore, and there was no way I could make it! I COULD NOT DO THE IMPOSSIBLE FOR MYSELF. And it was many years before I read for myself Jesus' statement, "With men this is impossible but with God all things are possible." It is HIS perfecting, not my own, which makes the great difference.

If I was excluded from God's family by my inability to fit into the fundamentalists' idea of God, then I decided I would have a fling at all that was worldly and forbidden. I would find a place where I could "fit in." And that is exactly what I did! I fit in. I found excitement and pleasure in a world of entertainment. As a musician and professional entertainer one can go to a party every night where he is the guest of honor and have a very wild time in the process.

I found alcohol gave the "high" I had never found elsewhere and all the shyness was suddenly replaced by a new kind of bottled boldness I had never known before. This was a "freedom" I had heard about but never found.

Certainly I was aware of the fact that one had to drink this boldness and freedom, but it didn't seem to matter at the time. This way of life continued for many years. It got faster and wilder, and I couldn't get off the merry-go-round because I did not know how to get off.

Since the only real freedom and peace is spiritual and is free, it is obvious that any other freedom and peace is artificial and is not free; it has a price. In my case the price was a fast development of a drinking problem which progressed right into the middle stages of alcoholism! If you know about alcoholism you will know without my telling it, and if you do not know, you cannot possibly understand this horrible addictive illness. A sickness of body, mind, and soul. I had a definite drinking problem at age 23 which continued until I was 39!

When I had enough and wanted help, I located a fellowship of men and women who share their strength, hope, and experience toward a spiritual recovery from alcoholism. They told me I must be willing to go to any lengths to be free of a drinking problem. And I was willing. They also had a magic phrase which followed the word of "God" in their writing and speaking. It said, "AS YOU UNDERSTAND HIM."

Nobody in my life had ever given me the right to my own concept or relationship with God. Always it had been someone else's concept of an angry God, anxious to punish, strict beyond measure, and with more rules than you could read in a lifetime. From my own experience I have always been careful to offer others this same personal and individual beginning contact with God. "As you understand him" is the only contact which will work for you. My concept may be of no value to you at all.

With my new God of LOVE, I began a process of spiritual growth, willing to go to any lengths to find peace and freedom. Certainly I put down the bottle and "gave up" alcohol. This was no big deal because it was killing me. But the only other "giving up" I had to do was of myself. A total and complete giving up of myself to the care of God, AS I UNDERSTOOD HIM.

From this total giving up, came a new spiritual experience and a joy and freedom which cannot be reduced to words. Only those of us who have been down the road of complete desperation and total loss can truly appreciate the restoration of our Lord and the real re-creation of every part of our person. This was FREEDOM IN CHRIST. And I never gave up a thing. It was all taken away as I kept seeking the reality of Christ in my life. It was no do-it-yourself perfection, because I am still the world's worst self-perfectionist. And I thank God daily for what I am, remembering too well what I once was!

At the end of about two years after my conversion and recovery experience I went to a town in western Texas to visit. I spent some time with an old and close friend with whom I shared drinks in years past. He never developed a drinking problem, even though we had tossed off more than a few in our time. Here I was very excited in sharing with him my freedom from alcoholism and my new relationship with God. And here he was just as excited in sharing his experience with the baptism of the Holy Spirit and praying in tongues!

This man was talking just like a card-carryin' "Holy Roller! " And I knew he was a member of a traditional church, a college graduate, member of the Country Club, and one of the older families in town. This was no kook or crackpot. Certainly no emotionalist, because I knew him well and his personality was quiet and shy. He related his experiences in a matter-of-fact way that made his experience seem the most natural and normal spiritual growth pattern I ever heard. In short, he turned me on to this experience as a reality where Pentecostals had turned me off for forty years!

He loaned me a copy of John Sherrill's book THEY

SPEAK WITH OTHER TONGUES, which I later loaned to someone else; and last I heard it was in Switzerland still making the rounds, with results only God knows about. As I read this book I got the same impression, that the baptism of the Holy Spirit is a natural and normal step in the Christian experience. I became more fascinated and more anxious to seek this experience as I read the New Testament again.

I knew no person in my own city who had had such an experience, so I went back out to the town in West Texas to ask more about my friend's experience. I knew the pastor of a local Pentecostal church, and I thought they had the local franchise, so I attended a Sunday service and went down front to seek whatever they had. Nothing happened! I think this was our Lord's way of telling me his Spirit is not franchised by any one group.

The next day we went to the home of a retired Methodist minister whose wife had an unusual ability to present this experience in the simplest and most direct terms. And it was there that I received the baptism in the Holy Spirit with praying in tongues. Me a "Holy Roller?" No dear, me an Episcopalian with a private and personal experience which leaps over barriers and has nothing at all to do with the church I was led to join.

Prayer in the Spirit is not an arrival point in Christian experience so much as a tool for travel. For me, it is not a badge to be worn as indicating some advanced state of grace. I still have a long way to go, and I am the first to admit it. For me, it has never been a performance one trots out to impress or entertain believers or non-believers, like playing the violin.

For me, this mystery experience is the strength to go another mile when I could not have gone otherwise. It has often been guidance when I had none. It is peace when my peace has been shattered by the problems of the day. It is the ability through prayer to do things I could not and would not do otherwise. It is depth and dimension in Christianity which I definitely need for the work I do and the problems I face. I do not pretend to understand what happens in the mystery of the baptism of the Holy Spirit. This does not prevent my use of the experience. I do not pretend to understand electricity. But this does not prevent my turning on my lamp for the light I need!

For seekers I feel the most important factor is a complete submission to God as you understand him, not necessarily the seeking of an experience itself. If we seek the Lord in all the reality we can, then he will lead us into those experiences which give us that reality.

I had few hangups about the experience. Because I had experienced such despair before our Lord changed my life, I had few reservations and was quite willing for God to make as many changes as he saw fit.

For those who have hangups, let me clear the air on a few: the baptism in the Holy Spirit will not make you some kind of far-out freak! People will not be able to point you out on the street or in your church and say, "Look at the funny holy roller!' " Certainly they will note a new depth in your Christian experience, but they will not be able to define it unless they have had a similar experience. It is a strange thing, but most people who have had this experience can and do recognize others who have had it, without a spoken word. I cannot explain this "inner witness." It needs no explanation.

The experience with the Holy Spirit does not mean you or I will leave our church to join another. I am a member of a traditional church and expect to remain so. My church says, "Within this broad framework you may have your own spiritual experiences," and that is exactly what I am doing. Because the experience makes you a better Christian, you will be a better Methodist, or Catholic, or Episcopalian. I did not, or do not run all over town passing out literature on the baptism in the Holy

Spirit. Like peace, deliverance, healing, or any of the other experiences in my life, I witness when I have definite leading to do so, and I remain silent when I do not have leading to witness. This experience has not been perfection in my life, but rather the power of prayer to seek our Lord's perfecting grace and growth.

I have once had to deal with the self-righteousness and a lack of love in my life AFTER the experience with the baptism in the Holy Spirit. And I once had the idea that this experience was a perfection itself and nothing would be needed beyond it. Again, it is a means of travel and not an arrival point.

Because I became willing to go to any lengths to find spiritual peace, I found new experiences with our Lord which were beyond my wildest expectations. I am an unusual person with unusual problems. The work I do with alcoholics is difficult and tiring. I could not possibly face the problems and unusual facets of my life now without the added boost of my private prayer life with the baptism with the Holy Spirit. I cannot "sell" anybody the baptism in the Holy Spirit. But for those who seek growth in the Christian adventure, it seems the next natural and normal step for the seeker.

I have found one peculiarity in having the baptism in the Holy Spirit! When I formerly was drunk with alcohol, those who didn't drink looked down at me. Now that I'm drunk on the "new wine" I've discovered that those who don't imbibe at the fountain of living water don't appreciate me either! Hallelujah!

DR. HONG AND AMY SIT
Pastor, Grace Chapel,
Houston, Texas

"When my wife Amy received, I was rather skeptical. I began to observe her life very closely, very critically. For example, whenever she burned the rice or failed to dust a little corner of a bookcase I would say, 'So you are baptized in the Holy Spirit, are you?' . . . I FAILED TO REALIZE THAT THEY HAD SO MUCH LOVE BECAUSE THEY SPOKE IN TONGUES."

Hong
Born in St. Louis, Missouri of Chinese origin. Both parents were born in China, but spent most of their lives in USA. Hong attended school in the U.S. except for one year in China in a Baptist high school. Attended the University of Illinois, majored in Chemistry. Graduated summa cum laude. Member of Phi Beta Kappa. Received BD and STM (Master of Sacred Theology) at Faith Theological Seminary, Wilmington, Delaware in 1950. Received Th.D. at Northern Baptist Seminary, Chicago, Illinois. Served in U.S. Army during World War II as a Captain in the Signal Corps, in charge of interpreting and translating at General Marshall's headquarters in Peiping, China. President of Chinese Foreign Missionary Union, which is the first mis-

sionary effort by Chinese Christians in modern times. Dr. Sit has pastored Baptist and independent churches and founded and pastored Grace Chapel, Houston, Texas, where he is pastoring at the time of this writing.

Amy
Amy was born in Foo Chow, China, the country which produced Watchman Nee, John Sung and Leland Wang (her father). When she was little, "Uncle" Watchman used to come around their house frequently. Her father, Leland Wang was often called "the Moody of China." She came to the United States to study to be a concert pianist, under a scholarship at Curtis Institute of Music (part of Curtis Publishing Company). This school specialized in producing concert artists. Graduate of Wheaton College of Illinois. She has been active in teaching women's seminars. She has written many singing scriptures and a number of songs. Has published four songbooks. Hong and Amy have four children.

We love to hear them talk as the Chinese accent flavors their language. You can almost hear the foreign tones in their writing as you read inside their hearts about their search for and discovery of POWER!

DR. HONG AND AMY SIT

Amy

About twenty years ago I received the baptism of the Holy Spirit; and I WAS A BAPTIST MINISTER'S WIFE. I knew that I was drying up spiritually, and I wasn't satisfied with my spiritual life. I knew that one needs to be filled with the Holy Spirit, so for about seven years before that I was reading every book I could get hold of about the baptism in the Holy Spirit. Well, every book tells you you need to be filled, and I was all convinced of it; but THEY NEVER TELL YOU HOW OR WHAT HAPPENS WHEN YOU ARE FILLED. So I'd try to tell myself that now I was filled. Then, something leaked away. Then it was the same old story again.

One night there was a young teen-age girl who came to me with a real problem. She was only fifteen years old, and she was talking acout committing suicide. I thought, "I haven't got a word for her." What I needed was the Holy Spirit for power and wisdom to know how to talk to her. That really brought up the urgency of it. I couldn't fill myself. I knew whether I was filled or not, and I KNEW I WASN'T filled with the Holy Spirit.

Then the Lord gave me a promise, "Seek and ye shall find. Ask and it shall be given you. Knock and it shall be opened unto you." I didn't know very much about the Holy Spirit at all, how you receive the fullness, but I just hung on to that promise. I said I'm going to keep on seeking until I find it.

That night after church we were all sitting around the kitchen table. We had a visiting minister, Henry and his wife Corrie. He was my husband's seminary schoolmate in a Presbyterian seminary. My husband would always say that Henry was a fine person and a smart student. The only trouble with him is that he speaks in tongues.

Once he just came out of the clear blue sky to visit us with all of his children, five or six or something like that. He came to the door and said, "Here we are." We were just completely surprised. So we asked him to speak at the church. It was a Baptist church. Something inside of me just said, "Henry has something that we don't have." I got more and more hungry.

I said that night while we were sitting around the kitchen table, "If Henry and Corrie would lay hands on me I believe I would receive the baptism of the Holy Spirit," although I really didn't know what it was all about. I told him that I felt so dry and I felt that I really needed to have this experience. But nobody did anything that night. We all got down on our knees and prayed, and Corrie and Henry said that they felt that the Lord would fill me in a few days or in the very near future.

All I wanted to know about the next day was the filling of the Holy Spirit. That's all I wanted to talk about; and I was crying and crying, as if the Lord was emptying me out.

The next night, I said, "I'm going to go to that prayer room in the church, and I'm not going to go to sleep tonight until God fills me with the Holy Spirit." We had four little children then, all babies. I said, "I'm going to put them all to bed, and I'm going to stay up all night if I have to." I went to the prayer room and said, "Lord, if you want somebody to pray with me, let them come. Otherwise, I don't want to call people to come to the prayer room."

I went there and lo and behold everyone (Henry and Corrie and my husband) all came to the prayer room. I didn't even tell them I was going to be there. They started coming in, and so we prayed. It was about midnight when the Holy Spirit came upon me. Instead of speaking in tongues right off the bat, I was prophesying. The Lord said, "Don't be afraid. You will bear fruit." Three times it just burst out of me, and I had never heard of people prophesying or anything like that.

I was satisfied. I felt that the Holy Spirit had filled me, although I didn't speak in tongues that night.

After a little while we went to a revival center somewhere. The Lord just led us there. That night, the minute I walked into the church, I started to cry again. The minister said, "God is going to give you the desire of your heart." He didn't know me or anything about me. I went in there and it was a strange experience, because before the sermon there were several prophecies. I couldn't even keep my eyes open the whole time. I just had my eyes shut, and I wasn't looking at anybody. Different prophecy was directed to me. I knew it was coming. It felt like an arrow flying all the way to where I was. The Lord gave me different prophecies. I told him, "This is a real privilege, and I can never love you enough." I made a real commitment to him that night! When the sermon started, it seemed as if he said, "Now you go up to the prayer room." The lady who came with me took me up to the prayer room where it was all dark. There was a man on the floor. He heard us, and he was going to get up. It was as if the Spirit wouldn't let him get up. So he put a handkerchief over his face. Nobody saw who he was and he just continued on. He was praying in tongues the whole time. This lady and I got on our knees.

That night when we had arrived somebody asked me if I spoke in tongues. I thought, "Well, the Lord will show me what to do in his own way, because I don't want anything strange or anything like that." Actually, nobody in our church had had this experience at all. We were the first ones.

This man was going on so fast it sounded like a machine gun. I said, "Lord, if you want me to speak in tongues, you've got to slow him down, because I don't even know how to go about it." So the man started slowing down. I was just praying silently; he couldn't hear me. . . He just slowed down.

I said, "Lord, my husband always says to check it out as to whether they speak the blood of Jesus or not, to make sure this is not the devil." The man started saying, "the blood of Jesus." I didn't tell him anything. I was just praying in my heart to the Lord. He said, "the blood of Jesus." He said, "Lai-nee-doe" in Chinese, which means, "Come here. Come here."

That sort of settled my heart. I thought, "Well, the Lord says to come here, and this is the blood of Jesus." So it couldn't be the devil. Then, in the middle of his prayer, it was as though he really prayed about a burden on his heart. In the middle of it he started to laugh and laugh. I had never heard anybody laughing like that. He was laughing in the Spirit. He laughed for about twenty minutes straight, and I thought, "I don't see anything funny, but that man sure can laugh, right from the bottom of his soul." In the middle of that I caught it. I was laughing, too. Then I started singing, "Hallelujah." I thought, "They can hear me two blocks away! " It was a supernatural voice. It was so strong and way up there, not like me at all. In the middle of singing "Hallelujah!! " my tongue started going real fast. I didn't even hear myself. All I knew was that my tongue was going fast, and later on I asked the lady next to me, "Did I speak in tongues?" She said, "You sure did! " I was completely unaware of it. That's how I got that experience.

After that I went home. My husband wasn't with me that time. Our church organist, who was in her sixties, stayed with me one time when my husband was on a trip, just to keep me company. For that ten days she was telling me how this minister would get the baptism in the Holy Spirit and that minister received and that minister's wife received. I just followed her like a puppy dog from room to room asking her, "Mrs. Evans, did you ever speak in tongues?" She said, "Yes." I thought, "She's such a nice lady. If she speaks in tongues, it must be all right." She was the one who had introduced me to this revival center, you see.

That night when we came back home I wasn't going to

say anything. My husband said, "You look like a cat that swallowed a canary." He said, "Now, just tell me yes or no, did you speak in tongues? That's all I want to know." I just didn't want to get up and say, "Yes, I spoke in tongues." I didn't want him to ever think that I was better off than he was! I told him that some will get it easier, but that the ones who take longer are more stable and they last longer. So it's not who is better and who is not!

Anyway I didn't want to just tell him. So I got down on my knees with fear and trembling and I told him the whole experience. One of the prophecies was that I would lay down my life for the Lord, and that was the part he didn't like. But I was happy! I was thrilled to think that the Lord would allow me the privilege to lay down my life for him. I felt so privileged.

After that we didn't say much about it, but I felt such a difference. The Bible would open up like a new book to me. I never did go to a seminary, but my husband went to a couple of seminaries and got a doctor's degree and all that. I began to say, "Honey, look at this." He would think, "How did she know about that? She never did go to seminary." It really provoked him, you know.

So, I'll let him tell how he got the baptism. It really made a difference in my life.

Hong

When my wife Amy received, I was rather skeptical. I remember that night in the prayer room I started thinking to myself, "I couldn't trust a single person in this room. They are all carrying on so, praying all at once for one thing. We Baptists don't do that!" Later I said to her, "I couldn't trust anyone in there but you, and now I wonder about you!" I thought she was getting too nervous, and after she had these wonderful experiences in the Holy Spirit I began to observe her life very closely, very critically, because there were so many misunderstandings on my part. I suppose many people have this type of a wrong notion. For example, whenever she burned the rice or failed to dust a little corner of a bookcase I would say, "So you are baptized in the Holy Spirit, are you?" I thought that meant perfection, but of course no one is perfect in this life. I imagine it made things hard for her. Still I knew that she had something more than she had before. I began to pray, and I said, "Lord, if this is real I want it." I would argue with her. I told her, "Look, I have read this thing in the Greek, in the original language of the New Testament." You're just reading it in Chinese language. She would say, "All right, but you don't have the same results they had." I said, "But, I don't need this. I don't need the tongues. I've been filled already; besides, tongues is the least one of the gifts. It is listed the last one of the nine." She said, "Remember the old Chinese saying, 'You go from shallow water to deep.' If you don't know the least how can you know any more?" Well, that's true, but I consoled myself with the thought that I didn't need tongues. I had graduated from tongues to love. You know, we can fool ourselves, I imagine, to think that we have a lot more love than we really have; but one of the most outstanding demonstrations to me of love came to me when I visited a little assembly in Waco. We were perfect strangers there, but the first time we got there, the old gentleman, Brother Ewing, who was the pastor, embraced me and kissed me on the cheek, and welcomed me like a long lost brother. I THOUGHT HE MISTOOK ME FOR SOMEONE ELSE. But he really meant it. They were so full of love there, and when they finally told us that they also spoke in tongues in this New Testament Church, I thought, "It couldn't be too bad, because they have so much love." I FAILED TO REALIZE THAT THEY HAD SO MUCH LOVE BECAUSE THEY SPOKE IN TONGUES.

As a Southern Baptist minister I was caught up in the regular routine. We had three services on a Sunday, a meeting every day of the week. Monday was a deacons' meeting, Tuesday was the men's brotherhood, Wednesday was mid-week service, Thursday was W.M.U., Friday was youth council, and Saturday was to get ready for Sunday. I was so busy I had no time to wait on the Lord. Those people could take time to receive God, but God had to knock me out with an appendectomy. It was an acute attack of appendicitis. About the middle of the day, after suffering all morning, I asked my wife to go call in her Spirit-filled friends who believed in healing. I said, "Let's see what they can do." The first one she called was a man who is now a missionary in Argentina.

At that time he was one of my chief helpers in the Baptist Church. He was a Baptist, so I trusted him; but he had also had this experience of the baptism in the Spirit. He came, and he prayed like a house on fire. He told me that laying hands on me was like laying hands on a block of wood. There was no corresponding response on my part, because I was kind of daring him. I said, "Okay, let's see what you can do. Let's see if it's real."

That evening they rushed me to the hospital, and the physicians operated without apology. I wondered, "If this thing were real, why didn't God heal me." Later I realized it was the only way God had of taking me out of my routine so that I could take time to wait on him. You know, I feel that God will always answer prayer for healing unless there is a higher purpose to be served by the delay, to his glory. In this case I was given an extensive leave by the church. I took advantage of it by going to this church in Waco and for three days did nothing but just wait on the Lord and pray. I went forward at every service, and they had about two services a day. I prayed. The third day I got desperate and decided, "I must receive or give it up." So I fasted and prayed.

A young brother stayed right with me all day long. It was his father who greeted me earlier. He was so happy, praying in tongues, singing in the Spirit. I envied him. I was so dried up. I tried to pray next to him. Though I had confessed many times, "I have been filled. I don't need the tongues," the promise of John 7:38-39 would speak to me, He who believed in me as the scriptures said, from his innermost being shall flow rivers of Living Water. THAT I DIDN'T HAVE.

The third day God graciously filled me! It's been a whole new dimension of living and of serving the Lord ever since. My father-in-law, Doctor Leland Wang, who has served the Lord for over fifty years and was quite well known in the fundamentalist circles, heard about our experiences and wrote to us sympathetically. "You have gone from a mountain to a molehill. Now all the doors will be closed to you," he said. (Since that time Jesus baptized him with the Holy Spirit, and he's been on a mountain-top ever since!)

We wanted to obey God, regardless of the results. But I must confess and praise God for this, that by his grace it has not been a molehill experience. He has opened more doors than ever before, and we have seen more results in a shorter time than we had when we tried to serve God, however sincerely, without the baptism experience. For example, he has given us much greater faith than we've ever had before. I think of the case of Paul writing to the Thessalonians. In I Thessalonians 2:13 (KJV) he said that, "For this cause also thank we God without ceasing, because, when ye received the word of God which he heard of us, ye received it not as the word of men, but as it is in truth, the word of God, which effectually worketh also in you that believe." That's what God enabled us to do. We began to believe God that whatever we say will come to pass.

We, by faith, started a new work in Houston called Grace Chapel, moved into a new house with hardly any money and just the promise of Philippians 4:19, which we wrote down on the application for a G.I. loan. The realtor didn't like it. He said, "You'll never get it that way." I said, "But we have no boss but the Lord." The loan came through. The Lord enabled us to move in.

It's a long story, but we've seen this over and over. He supplied money for a missionary trip. He gives us faith for healing and to see miracles take place. Didn't the Lord say, "Ye shall receive power when the Holy Ghost comes upon you. Then, ye shall be witnesses unto me!" We have had the joy of seeing the Lord pour out his Spirit in the many places he has sent us, Hawaii, Tahiti, Far East, Australia, New Zealand, as well as here in America. I praise God that the most wonderful blessings of the baptism in the Holy Spirit to me have been even beyond this matter of greater faith and revival and power. It is simply this, that I feel I have been drawn much closer to the Lord because of the fullness of the Spirit. Jesus said, "He shall glorify me." That's why he sent us the Holy Spirit, to fill us, that we might know Jesus in a greater glory. Before this I thought that some people are just "that way." They are blessed with an extrovert personality. That's why they are so outgoing and so happy. But now I realize that God can change your personality. He can fill every person with his Holy Spirit, and he can fill everyone with joy, with joy unspeakable and full of glory; and the half has not been told.

Amen.

DR. W. DOUGLAS FOWLER, JR.

"I didn't pick tongues, GOD DID! I'll serve notice on all Christians that if speaking in tongues is offensive to you, you'd better check who your Lord is! The Christians who don't stay drunk on the new wine are the Christians who have problems."

"But if your gift is that of being able to 'speak in tongues,' that is, to speak in languages you haven't learned, *you will be talking to God* but not to others, since they won't be able to understand you. You will be speaking by the power of the Spirit but it will all be a secret." I Cor. 14:2 (TLB)

One of the most exciting families we have ever met is the Doug Fowler family; Doug, Sue and their five children, ages 7 to 15. All have received the baptism of the Holy Spirit and talk in unknown tongues openly and freely in their home. When there is squabbling among the children, the Holy Spirit wells up in Sue and she loudly begins to pray in the Spirit. All of the children come running like a bunch of chickens to a mother hen the minute they hear her prayer language, because they know she is talking to

God by the power of the Spirit about their behavior. They all gather around her, raise their hands and pray in tongues, and THE ARGUMENT STOPS!

When they come home from school, if their mother isn't home, she leaves them a note instructing them of the various duties they are to perform such as washing out their lunch pails, etc., and at the bottom of the note it always says "NOW LIFT YOUR HANDS AND PRAISE GOD! " Their entire house is decorated with signs "JESUS," "LOVE," "JOY," "PEACE," "FAITH," and there are scriptures in every imaginable place in the house. The love of God just runs all through their house and spills out the door!

Since the same Holy Spirit dwells in all six of them, the same power is available to all. We don't find that everyone who has received the baptism has the same ministry or assignment from Jesus, but when God wants to use any believer who meets the full requirement of discipleship Christianity, he will give ALL the power necessary to perform. The Fowlers relate the night God told them he had anointed their children to pray for the sick. As the four children lined up across the front of the assembly, the little ones standing on chairs, the power of God fell on them. Scores were healed as they were slain in the Spirit, when the healing power flowed through their tiny hands!

Biographical Data

MD — Louisiana State University Medical School, New Orleans, La.

Interned at U.S. Naval Hospital, Jacksonville, Fla.

Surgical training at Confederate Memorial Medical Center, Shreveport, La.

Member Southeastern Surgical Congress; American Society of Abdominal Surgeons; American Trauma Society; Duval County Medical Society; Florida Medical Association; American Medical Association; Member of Candidate Group of the American College of

DR. W. DOUGLAS FOWLER, JR.

Surgeons.
U.S. Navy, 3 years
Elder in Beaches Chapel
International Director, F.G.B.M.F.I.
Frequent speaker and lay minister for Christian organizations, conventions, etc.

I'm here as an heir to the grace of God. A few years ago we were living our own life and doing our own thing. We thought we had things pretty well made. Then life began to close in around us. Our story is a story of deliverance from the world. God didn't deliver us from the world to take us out of the world. He delivered us from the world to set us back in it. This is really our testimony, and that's what basically the Lord would have me to share with you.

"Jesus, we magnify your name, the name that is above all names, the name that is exalted in the heavenlies and on the earth and under the earth and the name to which every knee shall bow. Jesus, when you ministered on this earth, the words that you ministered were Spirit and they were life. Jesus, you said that we could ask and receive from you and the words that we would minister would be Spirit and would be life. So, Father, in the name of Jesus of Nazareth, we ask you right now to supernaturally anoint this sharing so that these words may be words of Spirit and words of life to the reader. You said, Jesus, that the Spirit of the Lord was upon you to set the captives free, to loose the chains, to open prison doors. Father, we believe this is a time of the opening of the prisons. We believe this, Lord, and we receive it in the name of Jesus. Hallelujah! Praise God!"

There was a testimony a few years ago by a man who experienced this in a revival-type crusade in Korea, and it spoke to me so strongly about the supernatural power in Jesus in delivering from prison. His ministry was simply sharing as he told about having been in a crusade in Korea. In the crusade, it looked as though things weren't particularly going any special way; but he challenged them to find someone who was hopeless and to bring them to the crusade. They brought a little girl up to the prayer line who had been demon-possessed and who was completely out of control — a breathing, frothing, screaming maniac. She had never spoken naturally. She had never had any communication with her family, and she was for all intents and purposes hopeless with no way to receive the gospel. As he stood on the stage they drug this little girl out and shoved her into his arms. He threw his arms around her and held her. She struggled and even bit him on the chest. As he held her, she suddenly became still and calm; he didn't talk to her or anything but just let her go. As she stood there, the thought came to him, "I've never really talked to her about Jesus. There's no way for her to know and hear." She turned around, and he asked her, "Young lady, have you ever seen Jesus?" The little girl looked up to him, and in perfect understanding said to him, "Why yes, I was sitting in a prison, and Jesus walked in and opened my cell door. He said, 'Come out. I've set you free.' Sure I know him!" He said that the Spirit of the Lord fell on that place. The next thing he saw was a crutch sail across the stage in an arch. Then some little man who had been in a wheelchair was running up and down the stage.

The sovereign power of God can move into a life, into a home and into a family and bring an understanding of the ways of God so people can live above the circumstances of life. If I had a scripture that is my testimony, it would be this scripture in Isaiah where God asked a question, Isaiah 28:9. "Whom shall he teach knowledge? and whom shall he make to understand doctrine? them that are weaned from the milk, and drawn from the breasts. For precept must be upon precept, precept upon precept; line upon line, line upon line; here a little, and there a little: For with stammering lips and another tongue will he speak to this people. To whom he said, This is the rest wherewith ye may cause the weary to rest; and this is the refreshing: yet they would not hear. But the word of the Lord was unto them precept upon precept, precept upon precept; line upon line, line upon line; here a little, and there a little; that they might go, and fall backward, and be broken, and snared, and taken."

That's what God did with us. We were living our own life and doing our own thing. We thought we had things pretty well under control. I remember as a teenager in a Methodist Church in a revival, the Spirit of the Lord had moved on me, and I had gone to the altar and given my life to Jesus.

I never had any questions or problems in terms of my scientific education or any other problems in the world concerning my eternal relationship with God. That was something that did not frustrate me. The only problem with my situation was that here I was with an eternal relationship with God and no power here, no power in my home, no power in my life, no power to tell others about who could help them. My wife, Sue, had been raised in a Methodist background, and through the circumstances that exist in churchianity these days, had never been born again. The pressures of the world began to move in on our home. We were in the Navy stationed in Jacksonville, and we got involved in the circle looking for peace. When you are looking for peace, if you don't go to the Prince of Peace, you'll likely go to a bottle. If it's not a big bottle, it may be a little bottle with pills in it or some other substitute, looking for peace. It was in the midst of these circumstances a few years ago that God began to speak to us.

Now, it's never the will of God, if I understand it scripturally, for us to have to go down to the pit — to the bottom of the pit — to get help. The problem, of course, is that most of us won't listen until we get down to the bottom. Most of us have a lower nature which is a "pit dweller," and it takes these pit stops for us to hear the voice of God. So, on our way down to the pit, God began to try to help us out. Sue's mother, who was a Methodist over in Arkansas, began to send us little care packages of literature. They would include such things as testimonies about the baptism of the Holy Ghost and speaking in tongues and copies of Voice Magazine. Naturally, like good, intellectual people, we mocked these things and threw them in the garbage. The only problem was when we got down to the bottom of the pit, we remembered the word of the Lord, and we called for help. I called my mother-in-law. We were in a situation where, had I not been a physician, Sue would have been put in some mental hospital, because of the problem. I knew who she needed for help. I knew she needed the Lord, but I had no power to help her. I naturally had enough insight to know that she needed help, but we didn't know what to do. When we got down to the bottom, we called my mother-in-law to come over and help us. Your friends might not like it that you speak in tongues, but let one of them get sick and you're the first one they're going to call, because they know where the power is. We called her. She came over to our home. She looked at her daughter and said, "Sue, you need Jesus. When you get desperate enough, he's going to be there to meet you." In essence, she packed her bags and went back to Arkansas.

During a dramatic set of circumstances in our home, Jesus supernaturally came into the situation and Sue was born again! Many of the problems that looked like the bad things on the top of the pile began to settle down. There was enough measure of peace in that relationship that things looked as though they were going to level off pretty good. Of course, you realize that God the Holy Spirit is the administrator of God's business on the earth. God the Holy Spirit is the one who leads a person to Jesus. So, quite naturally, through the salvation relationship, every born-again Christian is aware of or knows the Holy Spirit. I run into people all the time who come up with such monkey business as telling me they have the Holy Spirit but they don't speak in tongues. It's important to realize that every born-again Christian does, indeed, know the Holy Spirit. The only problem about maintaining this relationship is that there's no way for the Christian to have power to stand against the work of the enemy. You may know the Holy Spirit. You may know your salvation. This is the situation we were in.

As things settled down in our home we were transferred, and I went into my specialty training in surgery. You must remember that I was quite religious to the extent that we never missed church services. They didn't do us any good, but we never missed. We were religious, and I was on the board of this and doing this and doing that in churchianity, and we were serving God. We thought that was what you were supposed to do — the typical pattern of churchianity. One man said he thought a nice way to do it would be to have it set up so that you got people in the church, got them saved, got them filled with the Holy Ghost, and then shoot them. Then, you'd have no backsliders.

Anyway, we were involved in situations and things. I don't speak critically. I thank God for my church upbringing and for the foundation that was laid. I thank God that this was God's blessing in my life, but I think it's important to realize that if God moves beyond where the anointing is in what we've learned in churchianity, and we don't move with him, we're going to be left behind. We're going to end up being an old shriveled-up, bitter, hateful snake with all kinds of meanness and resentment and bitterness and everything else living on the inside of us. I've seen it work. When God the Holy Spirit tries to move into a church or move into a family, there comes a point where we can resist the Holy Spirit only so long. Then, the anointing of God lifts and God leaves us in the hands of the tormenter. I've seen it happen. It's not that God doesn't love us. It's not that God isn't going to save us. I'm not talking about that. The purpose of the operation of the Holy Spirit in a Christian's life is not to get you to heaven, it's to get a little heaven to you. It's to teach you how to live heavenly here. This is the purpose. Jesus says that those who are the overcomers are the ones who are going to dance around the throne. I'll guarantee you, if you don't know how to dance around the throne here, you're not going to be able to dance around the throne up there. You're going to be ashamed. These are just some basic facts of life, and these are the things we learned.

Well, I was not exposed to any of these power things that were going on, because I was "Mr. Religious." I had everything I could ever want and had no desire for anything else. Sue went to a little home prayer group in south Arkansas held by some little Methodist lady. A man from Little Rock, Arkansas, came into their home and said God sent him there to pray for some young mother to receive the baptism of the Holy Ghost. Sue said, "That's me," and fell on her knees! This man walked over and put his hand on her head and she began to praise God in another tongue, not knowing anything about what the word of God had to say about this. She had no training or teaching about the baptism with the Holy Spirit. It was just that she was ready.

God sovereignly moved into her life and liberated my wife. Jesus is the only one who can liberate a woman. Women's Lib is from the pit. Women's Lib will get a woman into more bondage than she can ever get into on her own. Jesus is the only one who can ever liberate a woman, and my wife was a liberated woman. She blazed a hot trail of glory through southern Arkansas, northern Louisiana, and offended all of her family and all of mine.

I arrived home from the United States Navy late one evening at our home in Louisiana. I, "Mr. Methodist," was standing in the family room of our home, having never heard anything about the baptism in the Holy Spirit. My wife drove into the driveway, jumped out of the car, and walked into the family room. The door hit the back of the wall as she walked in. She got right up to my face and said, "Have you received the baptism of the Holy Ghost with speaking in tongues?" I said, "What?!! " I kind of backed off and said, "Now, I don't know what you're talking about, but I think you're crazy." I had enough of God in operation in me still left after all of my education and after all of my unbelief and after all of my religion that I told her, "If what you're telling me is in the scriptures, then I know that one day I'm going to have to answer to God Almighty for it. I've got to find out what you're talking about. I don't know what you're talking about. I'm ignorant." The Lord then began to work in my life. At that time I was involved in an upheaval situation in the natural — the beginning of a residency training program. To have a spiritual upheaval going on at home was something else.

God opened the door in my own home situation for me to have a little time to read the New Testament. I was at the point spiritually where I couldn't understand anything about King James English. Sue was completely set free, running around the house praising God, speaking in tongues and writing scriptures on the wall! She used to pick Bible promises out and say, "Oh! Oh! Glory to God! There's my word for the day." I was the one who was supposed to be spiritual, and I had to sit there and watch this sort of thing.

I took the New English translation of the New Testament that was at that time the most modern translation published. I said, "Now, God, I believe that if you are really sovereign, there's no translation of the scriptures that has ever been written that man could screw up. So I'm going to take the most modern translation (it happened to be that one at the time) and read it." Sure enough, the divine thread of God's truth ran right through those scriptures. That's why I don't worry about it when religious people start hollering about translations. Let me tell you something. One time God used a jackass to speak through. So any Bible that comes out as Bible, God can speak through. If you find somebody reading it, let them read it. Don't try to get them into some translation that you think is the perfect will of God, because God can use anything. That doesn't mean that I'm against sound teaching and instruction and understanding at all, but when a person has a need and God is speaking to them, God can speak through a jackass. Don't forget that.

God spoke to me in this translation, and I began to understand that what my wife was telling me was all true and that if I was going to come into a place where I was to have God's blessing in my life and in my family and in my home, this was the key. I went through, you might say, sort of a religious transformation that took about two or three weeks. It was about a month or two after Sue received that I also received the baptism in the Holy Spirit.

Let me say right here that if you've had an experience with the Holy Spirit that did not end in a new tongue, you've not been completely baptized.

That doesn't mean that you don't know him. But the Holy Spirit speaks. If you've had some experience with the Holy Spirit of feeling a tingle or whatever, and you don't have a new tongue, then don't leave without it, because the right Spirit has a tongue. The Holy Spirit is not a dumb spirit. Now, when I'm speaking of the baptism of the Holy Spirit, I'm speaking of the presence of God Almighty moving into a human life and teaching that life how to magnify God, teaching that life how to enter into a power relationship with him. The result is that the Christian will know how to pray and magnify God in his own prayer language!

The transformation I went through and went into was something like this! For about a week or two I told all of my friends, "I am certainly glad my wife has this. She needed it." Then, after that wore out (that was a lie, you know) I went around telling all of my friends, "Well, if God wants me to have this thing, he will do it." That was the biggest lie of all, because the last instruction that Jesus gave his disciples was to receive the Holy Ghost. The first thing Jesus did when he ascended on high was to send the Holy Ghost. He's never left. The book of Acts has never stopped. THE BOOK OF ACTS HAS NEVER ENDED. It's going to go on. Some people feel that in this day and age the book of Acts is going to look like a kindergarten primer by the standards we're seeing — the number of people turning to the Lord and the number of miracles God is bringing forth.

I hid behind that for a while. Then God began to draw closer and to deal with me. I thought my wife had conned me into going to a little meeting, but it wasn't her. It was God who had arranged it.

I think there were some Chinese missionaries that were teaching. At the end of the meeting, they said, "All right now, we're going to all raise our hands and praise the Lord." I thought, "No, I'm not. I'm a Methodist, and I don't behave like that." I got up and left the meeting!

I don't believe God has a set pattern for baptizing you with the Holy Spirit. God has an experience that is individual to all of his children, because there is a treasure in all of God's children. God knows just what it takes to get the treasure out. You've got scriptural signs or scriptural guidelines to tell whether you've got the right spirit or not. God had shown me scriptural teaching in the New Testament that in another tongue the flow of the Holy Spirit comes in the Christian's life. Speaking in tongues is one of the scriptural evidences that you've got the right spirit. You don't want an experience that doesn't have the right equipment with it, because if you don't allow God to give you the right equipment, eventually you will pick up a spirit of error. That's where things go wrong. I mean these technicolor vision sort of things that you see running around in little prayer groups and little metaphysical sort of trash. All of those things come in and seduce people who will not submit to the right spirit. These are guidelines Christians can go by.

Well, what happened to me was that I was riding home in the automobile. I came to a stoplight, and the voice of God began to speak to me. This was about seven or eight years ago now. God began to speak to me, and simply said, "All right, you call yourself a Christian. I'm offering you something that is in my word. I want you to know that from your standpoint you are rich and increased in goods and have need of nothing. I'm going to spew you out of my mouth." I remember sitting there in the car saying, "All right God, if that's the case, I'm fixing to get some of these tongues." Now, I didn't know how to speak in tongues, but I remembered how the natives in some of the movies talked. I remembered that was another language. I said, "All right, God here goes." I began to speak. I realized that as I began to speak that it was just as the scripture says, the Holy Spirit began to give the utterance. My mind was sitting back watching, "What are you doing? You're making all sorts of babbling noises. What's going on?" Of course, God's enemy came along right away and assured me that what was happening to me was not from God. Of course, I didn't realize that Satan can't even understand the tongue anyway. I realized that was a lie and that if I would continue to pray, the enemies of God would have to leave. I continued driving along speaking in tongues, and I knew it was genuine and that God understood what my spirit was saying!!

Speaking in tongues is a mystery to the one speaking because, like the Bible says, it's an unknown tongue or language. "For he that speaketh in an unknown tongue speaketh not unto men, but unto God: for no man understandeth him; howbeit in the spirit he speaketh mysteries." I Cor. 14:2. So when a Christian prays in an unknown tongue, he opens the doorway of supernatural communion with God the Father that the devil and all of his angels cannot understand, nor can any man understand. That's our holy personal relationship with the heart of God. That's the mystery of the tongue. I pray in tongues, not just because of the tongue, but because the Bible says I'm speaking the mysteries of God. What happens is when a Christian opens up his life to magnify God, to speak God's mysteries to him, God in return flows through him! Hallelujah!

God showed me right after I received the baptism of the Holy Spirit while sitting in my car — "This is not the gospel, this is Dr. Fowler's gospel." It sort of confirmed things to me — that my tongue was like a dam in front of a giant reservoir. You know how you run water over a dam through generators to get power. The Lord showed me that I would have just as much power as I let water run over the dam and that I would have just as little power as I let water run over the dam.

I'm here to testify as a physician that the only problems I run into with Christians in spiritual matters are Christians who don't pray in tongues enough. There is a reason for it. The baptism in the Holy Spirit and the speaking in another tongue is a new wine. When it first happened on the Day of Pentecost, do you remember they thought they were drunk, and it was nine o'clock in the morning! The importance of praying in tongues in the Christian's life is that this is the way for the Christian to get drunk on the power of the Holy Spirit.

The Christian who knows how to get up early in the morning and get drunk doesn't worry about his problems for the rest of the day. It simply works this way: "If you've got a man who has financial problems, what does he do? If he's a drunkard he goes to the bar and gets drunk. When he goes in he has a problem. When he comes out he doesn't have a problem. He may have given all of his money away to the rest of the drunks in the bar. He may hate somebody or the whole world when he goes into the bar and sits down at the barstool and gets the first drink. But after he gets two or three under his belt, the next thing he knows he is inviting some unknown character, maybe somebody from another race, down at the other end of the bar, 'Come on down here and have a drink with me.' The principle involved is that if Christians would drink enough new wine, they wouldn't be defeated by the problems of the world. We would be able to float above them. You see, a drunk doesn't worry about it when things don't go right. A drunk doesn't worry about his feelings. He gets drunker, doesn't he? A drunk doesn't worry about his hates. He drinks them away. A drunk doesn't worry about his financial problems. He just goes and gets drunk and buries his financial problems. The baptism of the Holy Spirit and drinking the new wine, praying in an unknown tongue as the scripture says, is the way for the Christian to get the overcoming power that he needs to face the problems of the world."

I am here to testify to you in the name of Jesus that if I had not learned how to operate in the power of God in this day and age, within the past month I would have been in a place where it would have been nothing for me to have listened to a suicide demon and take a gun and shoot myself, because of persecution that had arisen. It's a sobering thing, but just a gist of some of the persecution is this. There was a complaint filed against me as a doctor at one of the hospitals where I operate. I operated on a young girl in whom we found a breast cancer. I told the girl I was going to pray for her. Some rumor got started, and someone filed a complaint against me as a physician, because I told the patient I was going to pray for her. I got called before a disciplinary board at that hospital. Now, I know what it is to stay drunk. Let me tell you what happened. When I got that letter from that disciplinary board, I sobered up in about thirty seconds. Then, the voice of God spoke to me and said, "I delivered Shadrach, Meshach, and Abednego from the fiery furnace; and I delivered Daniel from the lion's den. It's nothing for me to deliver you." So I just kept on drinking new wine. What I think about drinking this new wine is that when you get to drinking, a little dab will not do you. There's one thing I would say to all of you in dealing with people's problems and in dealing with problems of today, THE CHRISTIANS WHO DON'T STAY DRUNK ARE THE CHRISTIANS WHO HAVE PROBLEMS!

There's some kind of a funny doctrine going around in the body of Christ that you don't pray in tongues unless the anointing "comes on you" to pray in tongues. Let me tell you, that is unscriptural. Paul said in I Corinthians 14:15, "I will pray with the spirit, and I will pray with the understanding also." You don't pray with your understanding just when the anointing comes on you. You pray because you need to. So the reason for praying in tongues is not because the anointing of God swoops down and makes you do something. I pray in tongues because I need to.

When I am faced with a problem and a trial, the anointing of God is not there. So I get drunk! That's the principle. If we Christians would learn this operation, then we would be able to overcome many of the problems the enemy throws at us.

By and large if a Christian will take the power of God when he gets up in the morning and get good and drunk on new wine, then he will have power to operate during the day against the work of the evil one. The disciple John did. He got up on the Lord's Day and got *"in the Spirit"* — he got drunk on new wine. (from Rev. 1:10) This is the principle that is involved in the baptism of the Holy Spirit.

The baptism of the Holy Spirit with the evidence of praying in tongues is our Spirit-given means of perfect communication with God.

One of the most dramatic miracles of my life occurred when I prayed with my spirit: An announcement came over the loudspeaker that our awaiting plane had two flat tires. I considered renting a car to drive the fifty miles in order to fulfill my speaking engagement. As I was standing at the counter a lady came up and sort of pushed me aside and said, "Let me have those keys." She grabbed the keys and said, "I've got to drive back over to Mobile now." She turned to me and said, "Young man, would you like a ride?" I said, "Yes, praise the Lord! " As we left the station she turned to me and said, "Young man, I'll have you know I never pick up hitchhikers." I said, "Well, glory to God, you didn't know Jesus had you drive over here to pick me up, did you?" She laughed. In the car she began by telling me she was a Jew of Jews and had been raised in a synagogue. She talked on and on about the synagogue, about owning a chain of interior decorating firms, about her husband's recent death and about her children having problems with drugs. As she was telling me about being a Jew, I said, "You know, I know your brother real well." She said, "Oh, is that right? Who?" I said, "Jesus." She said, "Well, you know in the synagogue they used to tell us that he didn't walk on water, but I never did believe that."

As I was driving with this woman, the Spirit of the Lord began to prompt me to pray in tongues! I didn't want to do anything out of order. I wanted everything to be done properly and under God's design, and I didn't want to make a fool of myself. So I just asked the Lord to show me what was going on. He said, "Ask this woman if she would like to pray." I asked her and she said, "Oh, I would LOVE to pray! " I said, "Praise God! Did you know that Jesus could give a person another language for praying to God and praising him? It goes something like this." I began to speak in an unknown tongue for this lady. At the time we were driving in front of the battleship Alabama, and as I began to speak these words, her mouth flew open. She pulled the car to the side of the road, stopped, and looked at me and said, "Young man, how do you know Hebrew?"

I said, "Lady, I don't know any Hebrew." She said, "Well, you just told me in Hebrew that as a daughter of Zion I must stop and see God. I know now that I love this Jesus!" Praise God for confirming the genuineness of unknown tongues and his sovereign way of drawing one of his chosen children to Jesus.

Had I not prayed in the Spirit, to be drunk enough for the Holy Spirit to use me, I would not have had the power to allow the Spirit to flow through me to bring light to her. The Bible says when one sinner repents all of heaven begins to rejoice. That Jewish lady in front of that battleship there on that highway turned heaven on in that instant, because of this Holy Spirit given ability. If you have received the Holy Spirit you have been given a tongue. So just get drunk on the new wine and stay drunk! The problems with some Christians is they just don't drink enough of that new wine!

The only Christians that cool down are the ones that get sober. I can testify to you that the anointing of God and the presence of God and the power of the Holy Spirit is greater today than it was when we first came into this new dimension of the Spirit.

Little Suzie had an incurable disease, Cystic Fibrosis. As Methodists we didn't know anything about healing. I was a doctor. I had done everything medically I knew for her. We began to learn about God's healing power. We learned from the word of God that Jesus was beaten before they hung him on the cross, that they gouged out his flesh and tore it off with the Roman whip. We discovered that "by his stripes we are healed." By those stripes he had paid the price for our healing. That means that it is already an accomplished, settled fact! God is more interested in Christians staying healthy than in their being healed! I believe if we Christians would stay drunk we would stay healthy, and all of our infirmities would flow right out the window.

It doesn't mean that we're not going to be attacked. We've been attacked. There have been times when God has sovereignly moved in our family and taught us and moved instantly into divine health, and there have been times when God has not healed us. We've had to learn to walk by faith. We've had to learn to walk step by step with diseases. Suzie had this problem; we didn't know what to do. She was about four years old at the time, and she came up to her mother one morning after having had a real bad attack. She said, "Mommy, you haven't asked Jesus to heal me." We knew this was God's time. We put our hands on her little chest and said, "Thank you, Jesus, for healing her. Thank you that when you died on the cross you paid for this." That child coughed once and to this day has never wheezed again. She is a completely normal, healthy fourth grader.

When Abigail was a new-born baby, she developed infant diarrhea and a dehydration problem and was in a coma. We were infants in the Bible at that time. I knew that as a physician I could do this or that for her, but I knew that medically speaking there was not a cure for her problem. I knew Jesus was her healer. I was on duty at the hospital and Sue was at home holding the fort. I'd get a little bit of unbelief and tell her to bring her to the hospital. Sue would say, "No, it's not time." While we were talking back and forth on the phone, the child kept getting worse and worse and worse. I kept having all sorts of thoughts: "What if she dies? What are they going to say if a doctor's child dies?" Late one night in the hospital I remember falling on my knees, and the Spirit of God began speaking to me. He said, "Whose child is she?" I said, "She's yours, God! You created her. You gave her to me to keep, but she's not mine. Well, God, all right, I understand. That child is yours, yours to keep. You can take her. Take her!" Just as I said "take her" I saw, in a vision, Jesus sitting on a throne with our child in his lap. I saw an angel, a big radiant angel, standing at his left side. From that instant, in the wee hours of the morning, our child was completely healed! She got up playing the next morning, had not had a drop of fluid, and was completely healed as if nothing had ever been wrong with her!

We've learned to teach our children how to operate by faith. When they get hurt and come to us with their problems, we've learned to ask them, "Do you want healing, or do you want pity?" Sometimes they just want pity. If they've got some desperate need that hasn't been met and they just want attention, that's what God will give them. But they've learned by experience that it's no fun to take that route, that the real blessing is in health. They've learned to pray for one another. I guarantee you, when you get a two-year old that prays for you, you'd better get healed, because he's believing!

It's so simple for a child to come into the baptism of the Holy Spirit. Jesus said unless you become as a little child you can't get the things of the kingdom of God. All of our children pray in the Spirit. Part of our daily routine in evening prayers is to get on our knees and pray with our understanding and pray with our spirit. This doesn't mean that children don't know that there is that time in their lives where they have to make the decision to walk with God. Young people face this. Our older children are just now understanding this. I believe the key to teaching young people how to walk with God is to teach them the principles of the kingdom of God. The word of God says that the kingdom of God is not meat and drink, not doing your own thing, but righteousness, peace, and joy in the Holy Ghost. It's easy for a young person to understand that if he wants to do his own thing he forfeits the kingdom of God. If he wants to do his own thing in rebellion, then God will leave him in the hands of the tormentor. But once he's tasted the kingdom of God, it doesn't take an idiot to learn where the goodies are. That's what our young people are learning. They learn how to stay in the kingdom of God. There are times when they choose not to, and that's when the rod of direction has to help them stay there.

We recently had a man come to visit us, a minister in a Christian church. He was like Nicodemus, sneaking out at night. He pastored a little church, sort of like Lazarus' tomb. He didn't have a whole lot of members, but it was his church. He said he heard that we were in the move of God, and said, "I want to get my church moving into the things of God." I sat down with him and said, "Do you know what you are asking for? In the first place, you need to realize that you're going to lose everything you've got. In retrospect you'll look back on it and realize that you didn't have anything to begin with, but a little religious club. But, if that's your kingdom, if that's where your security is, then you'd better check it out, because you're going to lose everything you've got, because when God moves into a church, he's going to take it over. You're going to have every Tom, Dick, and Harry flowing into your church. You're going to see the most desperate of needs. That's where God is, where the needy are. God is not where the full are. God is where the needy are. Until you can stand at the altar of your church and speak to a need and say, 'In the name of Jesus, Shum ba la ta ka,' God will never move in your church." "Well," he said, "I'm ready."

He came back the next week to see me, and he had his nice little religious argument against speaking in tongues in relation to the baptism in the Holy Spirit. You see, the only problem people have with the Holy Ghost is "tongues." Tongues is the only thing, because to the objectors it's offensive. I didn't pick tongues, God did! I'll serve notice on all Christians that if speaking in tongues is offensive to you, you'd better check who your Lord is!

Every time a preacher gets up and preaches against tongues, more people receive the Holy Ghost. The simple fact is that you just can't stop God's move. I don't have any bitterness about this, I simply think it is important to be wise and to realize what is going on. God is moving! God is drawing a people! God is going to have a people that will follow him all the way!

This minister came back to the religious argument that tongues had passed away and had stopped with the apostles and the usual theological things that they learn in "cemetery." I sat there and rejoiced. He said, "Now show me in the scriptures what you're talking about." So I took the word of God and walked through the scriptures with him. He saw! Then he began to confess that he had received the baptism in the Holy Ghost and prayed in tongues. "Praise God! Now, you've got to get yourself free if you want God to move."

I later took him with me to a Methodist Church where they have a little Friday meeting. As the Spirit of God was moving in prayer, the Lord had me call him up to help minister. Once that brother got to tasting the goodness of God he was louder in tongues than I was!

God is moving. God is going to have a people who will move with him. God wants every day in our lives to be filled with his power. He wants us to have such a walk with him that our daily lives are filled with miracles. Miracles are not to be an unusual circumstance of life. They are to be the daily events of Christianity. This was the walk of Jesus. Jesus said that greater things than he did on earth we would do. So in this day and age we ought to see more miracles than we read in the Bible. Miracles did not pass away.

Somebody asked me the other day if I went to see the movie "The Exorcist." I said I wouldn't go see that kind of trash, that if they wanted to see exorcising of spirits they could come to my office. I do that as a part of my daily work — the *right* way. A woman came in my office the other day crippled with arthritis and stiff joints and couldn't move. She actually came to me because she thought I was a wizard or some kind of spiritualist. She thought I practiced witchcraft, and that's what she came for. She had been in Edgar Cayce and all that occult trash. In the examining room I started talking to her about Jesus. The Lord showed me that there was a demon of witchcraft that she had picked up. I talked to her, prayed with her, and told her to go home and burn her witchcraft stuff and come back the next week. She came back. I prayed with her and cast that demon of infirmity and witchcraft out of her. She got up and walked out of the office healed — well! That's the right way to cast out a demon! That's the scriptural way!

I had an experience a few months ago. A young fellow was shot on the beach and was brought in with a gunshot wound to the chest . . . I was not on call, but they just "happened" to call me. I got up and went to the hospital to see this kid. We rushed him to the operating room and operated on him. He was shot through the left ventricle, the lung, the diaphragm, the liver, the spleen, and the stomach. We repaired the ventricle, drained the lung, and repaired the diaphragm, took out a piece of the liver, took out part of the stomach and closed it, took out the spleen, and even found the bullet in this case, which you don't usually do except in a T.V. story. As we were getting this kid off the operating table, he died. He went into an electrical cardiac arrest — no electrical activity whatsoever in his heart. Several of us working with him did all the things you usually do to try to promote a survival in someone. Nothing was working. After about thirty minutes we were getting ready to cut off all the equipment and quit. God says, "Having done all, stand." So, I, having done all, stood. I stood by his bed and prayed in tongues. When I began to pray in tongues, this kid sat straight up in the bed, pulled his intra-tracheal tube out, and do you know what he said? "WATER! " I thought of how Jesus said, "if any man gets thirsty, let him ask me for a drink — out of his belly shall flow rivers of Living Water."

That boy was raised from the dead and went home in five days, healed!! Now, what do I care if somebody comes to me and tells me that "tongues" aren't real. That's ridiculous! When someone comes to you and tells you that you can't speak in tongues, that it has all passed away, you just keep on speaking. Okay?

God is looking for a people who will hear his voice and who will allow him to operate in them. When I'm dealing with patients, I don't pray with every patient that comes to see me. I have some patients that come to me with strictly medical problems, and we handle them. That doesn't mean that I don't lift up Jesus to them. That doesn't mean that I don't seek the doors to be open to witness. It's not some sort of a "preachy" situation. God settled the issue in my life about where I was supposed to be when we received the Holy Spirit. God showed me that I was to be planted in the kingdom of medicine as a light. I've got an answer when medicine runs out. That doesn't mean that every person that I deal with survives. That's God's business. I learned a long time ago that when Jesus rose from the dead and sat down at the right hand of the throne of God, one of the things God handed him along with his crown was the keys of life and death. I don't hold those keys. That's the greatest deliverance I had as a doctor, realizing that I'm not responsible for life or death. I'm responsible to minister to needs and do the best I can, but Jesus holds those keys. There are times when I've seen God sovereignly raise people from the dead and have seen God deliver and heal people supernaturally. There have been other times that I've seen people die. I don't have all the answers.

But I know this. There is a place in the heart of God where a believer can come to God with a need, and the power of God can sovereignly and supernaturally solve the need to the glory of Jesus. God is looking for a people who will allow themselves to get in the Spirit, to get drunk enough on new wine that he can flow in and out freely with power and authority. The Bible says the glory of God is going to fill the earth as the waters fill the sea. Do you know that about half of the Christians would be scared to death if the glory of God came on this earth? We are going to have to be drunk, or we're not going to be able to stand it. It will scare us to death. The Bible says that "God has not given us the spirit of fear; but of power, and of love, and of a sound mind." (II Timothy 1:7)

The baptism of the Holy Spirit, Christians, is to get us into the place where we can stand boldly and proclaim the name that is above all names, where we are, whatever we are doing. That's the purpose of the baptism of the Holy Spirit. It's not to get you to heaven. Jesus is the way to heaven. It's not to solve your problems. It helps, but the baptism in the Holy Spirit is to give the Christian the anointing or boldness that it takes to stand up against the work of the enemy and proclaim that JESUS CHRIST IS KING OF KINGS AND LORD OF LORDS!!!

Note: All references in this testimony are from the King James Version.

WHO, HOW, WHY?

Who is the baptism of the Holy Spirit for? It's for EVERYONE!
The BAPTISTS are receiving,
  the CATHOLICS are receiving,
   the BRETHREN are receiving,
    those from the CHRISTIAN churches are receiving,
     and so are those from the CHURCH OF CHRIST and the CHURCH OF GOD.
      Those from the COVENANT and C.M.A. churches are receiving.
       The EPISCOPALIANS are receiving,
        the FRIENDS are receiving,
         the LUTHERANS are receiving,
          the MENNONITES are too!
           The METHODISTS are receiving,
            the NAZARENES are receiving,
             the PENTECOSTALS are receiving,
              the PRESBYTERIANS are receiving,
               the REFORMED churches are receiving,
               even the ASSEMBLY OF GOD finds an occasional one who hasn't received the

baptism.

People from all kinds of non-denominational churches and prayer groups are receiving the power of God in their lives. God didn't say the baptism was for just a few, HE WANTS EVERYONE TO HAVE POWER IN THEIR LIVES.

This is God's hour of power, just as was predicted centuries ago by the prophet Joel, " 'In the last days,' God said, 'I will pour out my Holy Spirit upon all mankind, and your sons and daughters shall prophesy, and your young men shall see visions, and your old men dream dreams. YES, THE HOLY SPIRIT SHALL COME UPON ALL MY SERVANTS, MEN AND WOMEN ALIKE, and they shall prophesy.' " (Acts 2:17-18 TLB)

As we've had the fun of typing and editing these testimonies as they have come to us, we have cried and laughed with each one. We had asked God to bring testimonies to speak to the hearts of people of all faiths about the mighty power of God through his Holy Spirit baptism.

You may be a Catholic and God may use a Baptist to reveal the magnitude of this POWER for you.

You may be a Nazarene and God may speak to you through a Methodist's testimony.

You may be a Lutheran and God will use the testimony of someone from the Church of God to speak to you.

Because we asked God to put his chosen testimonies in this book, we believe God will open multiplied thousands of "spirit mouths" and pour into them his righteousness through the baptism of the Holy Spirit. "Open your mouth wide and see if I won't fill it. You will receive every blessing you can use! " (Psalm 81:10 TLB)

Why should we try to operate differently than Peter, James, John and the others? There is no reason, and there is no difference in the power, and the way the power is evidenced in the life of the believer. You'll notice some of the testimonies indicate they needed instruction before

WHO, HOW AND WHY?

God could fill their mouths.

We didn't know how to be saved until somebody told us.

"But how shall they ask him to save them unless they believe in him? And how can they believe in him if they have never heard about him? And how can they hear about him unless someone tells them?" (Romans 10:14 TLB)

Somebody told us *how* to be saved, but JESUS SAVED US!

We didn't know how to receive the baptism of the Holy Spirit until someone told us. He told us *how*, but JESUS BAPTIZED US! The same thing is going to happen to you if you really love Jesus and want all he's got for you. Remember that we're looking at an event in history some 2,000 years ago, and the same thing is going to happen to you in exactly the same way, RIGHT NOW! It's not going to be any different than the original time, because God hasn't changed and neither has Jesus!

The Holy Spirit was given one time to 120 people. Now the same Holy Spirit is going to be given to YOU. Right now while you read this, the Holy Spirit is already drawing near to you. He is engulfing you while you are reading this, enveloping you with his love and his power. Open your heart to receive ALL of him.

THEY began to speak. THEY gave the sounds of their voices and the Spirit gave the utterance, or language. And if you give the sounds of your voice, you're going to get sounds back, but this will be the language from the Holy Spirit.

Many of you will be hearing little sounds right now running through your mind. Strange little parts of words. Strange little syllables. You don't understand them, but listen for them, because this is the beginning of your Spirit language. Some of you may not hear anything, but will just begin to speak in a moment.

We're going to ask you to join with us in a little prayer in just a moment and in that second of time, in that instant, think of Jesus laying his hands on you to impart to you the gift of the Holy Spirit.

We want you to also remember that you can't speak two languages at one time. You can't speak in English and in your prayer language, so after we pray this prayer, we're going to ask you NOT to speak in English any more. And remember that all languages are made up of a bunch of mixed up little syllables, so give the Spirit some syllables so HE CAN GIVE YOU THE LANGUAGE. Remember the supernatural miracle is not a new set of vocal chords; the supernatural miracle is the language which the Holy Spirit gives you through your own vocal chords.

We have also discovered that if you will pray rapidly at first it will help you considerably because when you pray slowly you have a tendency to think about what's coming out of your mouth. When you pray in the Spirit, it has to bypass your mind, and you'll find this easier if you will pray a little faster.

If you just sit there and don't give any sounds, you won't receive anything back, because only if you give will you get! Remember also that the Bible doesn't say you will receive an emotional experience, but it does say you will receive POWER! Don't look for the emotional experience, look for the POWER! Some people do have an emotional experience, but not always. Many times the emotion will come AFTER you pray in the Spirit!

Every once in a while, someone will say, "I'm not going to make some silly sounds, the Holy Spirit's going to have to do it all!" May we remind you that God is a gentleman, and he will never FORCE himself on you, and so you, like those in the upper room on the Day of Pentecost, are going to have to do the SPEAKING! Once you're saved, the only thing that can keep you from receiving is YOU, yourself, if you don't open your mouth and speak!

WHO, HOW AND WHY?

The most important thing to know before you receive the baptism of the Holy Spirit, is that you are saved, so we're going to ask you to pray a simple little sinner's prayer right now:

"Father, I want to KNOW I'm saved, so I ask you to forgive ALL my sins. I believe that Jesus is your divine Son. I believe that he shed his blood on a cross for my sins. I open the door to my heart and I invite Jesus to come in. Take my whole life and make me the kind of person you want me to be. Now, Father, I thank you for hearing my prayer. I thank you for forgiving my sins. I thank you for saving me."

Let's pray again shall we? Remember that this is the great Holy Spirit of God we're going to receive right now. Are you ready?

"Dear Jesus, I believe the power of the Christian life lies in the baptism with the Holy Spirit, so I ask you to baptize me right now with the Holy Spirit. Fill me up from the bottom of my feet to the top of my head.

(Just wait for a moment now and feel him just filling you up, and filling you up, and filling you up.) Lord Jesus, I thank you because you've done your part; now I'm going to do my part. I'm going to open my mouth, and I'm going to give you some sounds and by faith I'm going to believe that the Holy Spirit is going to give me a language. Lord Jesus, I was saved by faith, and by faith I accept the baptism of the Holy Spirit. Because I trust you, Lord Jesus, I thank you in advance for the language the Holy Spirit has already given me. I love you, Lord Jesus. I worship you, Lord Jesus. I praise you, Lord Jesus. I magnify your holy name, Lord Jesus!

NO MORE ENGLISH! Now look up to God, OPEN YOUR MOUTH AND LET THOSE SOUNDS COME OUT *PRAISING GOD* and listen for that beautiful language the Holy Spirit has given you.

RECEIVE YE THE HOLY GHOST!

Keep praying, and really let it flow in long sentences.

Now that you've received, may we suggest that you PRAY MUCH IN THE SPIRIT! Pray at least 10 to 15 times a day in the Spirit! THE MORE YOU PRAY IN THE SPIRIT, THE MORE POWER WILL COME INTO YOUR LIFE. Sing in the Spirit — the Holy Spirit will give you tunes as well as the words! You have not been given God's Holy Spirit just to speak one time, but you can stop and start at will. You do not have to wait for the Spirit to "come on you," because the Spirit is now IN you, and so you can speak any time you want to in your new tongue. "And the spirits of the prophets are subject to the prophets." (I Cor. 14:32 KJV) A wonderful way to start off a day is to start off "in the Spirit!" When you wake up in the morning, don't pray in your native language, but start praying in tongues before you even get out of bed. You'll be amazed what this will do to your day!

The devil is going to come and visit you, just like he does everyone who receives. He can't understand tongues, so he can't stand them! He'll come sneaking around and tell you you're just making sounds, that it's just a bunch of gibberish. GET RID OF HIM WITH A SHORT, LOUD BURST OF TONGUES!!!

Right now we want you to do something else. Do you have a loved one who is unsaved? If so, put that person in the palm of your hand and hold your hand up to God and pray for that person in your NEW TONGUE! Pray softly and believe for a miracle. Recently at a meeting, a Jewish convert who had just received, placed her mother's name in her hand and prayed in tongues for her. That night about two o'clock in the morning, her mother called and said, "God's been dealing with me all evening. I've got to accept Jesus as my Messiah. Will you pray with me?" Thank you, Jesus!

You may start off with a little baby language, but just

WHO, HOW AND WHY?

keep on. Remember when your children were small they started out with a very small vocabulary, and then as they added new letters to it, they were capable of making more words. The same thing is sometimes true of your Spirit language. The Spirit can only give back to you what you give to him, so put those extra sounds of the alphabet in and see what he does with them! Don't keep on speaking a baby language, but allow the Holy Spirit to develop a full language in and through you.

The baptism of the Holy Spirit means *you have received power* — God's power. All the power you will ever need to do anything God ever tells you to do. DID YOU HEAR THAT? ALL THE POWER YOU WILL EVER NEED TO DO ANYTHING GOD EVER TELLS YOU TO DO! That's a lot of power!

What are you going to do with this power? How can you apply it? What is its final purpose?

TO PLEASE GOD AND JESUS!

The principal ingredients for abundant earthly life and for eternal life are:

1. Salvation (new birth, but continued victoriously until the end of our time) — TO PLEASE GOD AND JESUS!
2. Baptism with the Holy Spirit for POWER — TO PLEASE GOD AND JESUS!
3. Commitment — 100% of our lives — TO PLEASE GOD AND JESUS!
4. Bible — meditate at least an hour a day — TO PLEASE GOD AND JESUS!
5. Pray — about everything, continuously (think to God and hear him and obey) — pray with your understanding or mind (your native tongue language) and with your spirit (your unknown tongue) — TO PLEASE GOD AND JESUS!
6. Bear fruit — add souls to God's Kingdom; bear fruit — the fruit of the Spirit (Galatians 5:22-23) — TO PLEASE

GOD AND JESUS!
7. Witness — tell everyone you can about Jesus and how to get to heaven. The Holy Spirit in you will cause you to WANT to talk about Jesus, so be obedient to each opportunity and impulse — TO PLEASE GOD AND JESUS!
8. ACT — become a New Testament book of Acts in your own way in your own world. Meditate hundreds of hours in Acts (as well as the rest of the Bible) to see what Jesus and his disciples did and how they did it, and "go thou and do likewise" — TO PLEASE GOD AND JESUS!

WHY SHOULD "I" SPEAK IN TONGUES?

TO PLEASE GOD AND JESUS!